Oct 2010

"Ed Takes and Recovery Gives"

Warmly.
Cheryl

D0283141

TELLING ED NO!
*and Other Practical Tools to Conquer Your Eating Disorder
and Find Freedom*

WHAT PEOPLE ARE SAYING

"Cheryl's work is honest, forthcoming, and ultimately, hopeful. She shares intimately her battles with her own mind, her therapists, and her eating disorder, but shows how persistence and commitment to self lead to true recovery. With not just stories, but clear outlines of recovery tools and lessons learned from each chapter, *Telling ED NO!* is educational, practical, and an inspiring story of triumph."

Kirsten Haglund, Miss America 2008

"*Telling ED NO! and Other Practical Tools to Conquer Your Eating Disorder and Find Freedom* is a raw, honest look at the harsh inner dialogue that goes on inside the mind of someone with an eating disorder. Cheryl Kerrigan poignantly illustrates the sharp contrast between the chains with which ED enslaves and the freedom that Recovery gives. Like a trusted friend, Cheryl gently takes the reader's hand, persuasively encouraging a practical path toward healing, health, and wholeness."

Sari Fine Shepphird, PhD
Clinical psychologist and author of *100 Questions*
and Answers about Anorexia Nervosa

"Eating disorder survivor Cheryl Kerrigan shares her own day-by-day, step-by-step recovery journey in *Telling ED NO!* for one purpose—to prove to us that we can each be heroes in our own lives. When seen through Cheryl's eyes, asking for help becomes not a weakness but a unique source of strength. Cheryl also dedicates significant time to guiding us through techniques to tune out ED's voice and tune in to a new, fresh, and powerful voice—the voice of recovery. *Telling ED NO!* is a timely and refreshing reminder that YES, doing the hard work of recovery really is worth it! Bravo, Cheryl!"

Shannon Cutts
Author of *Beating Ana: How to Outsmart Your Eating Disorder and*
***Take Your Life Back* and Founder/Director of Mentor Connect: Where**
Relationships Replace Eating Disorders
www.key-to-life.com

"*Telling ED NO! and Other Practical Tools to Conquer Your Eating Disorder and Find Freedom* is a must read for anyone struggling with an eating disorder. Cheryl's humor and honesty helps foster understanding and provides support to individuals as they face the real challenges of recovery. Cheryl's willingness and courage makes the journey feel less daunting and will help all feel supported and less alone. Additionally, *Telling ED NO!* can provide family members with useful information and help individuals understand the seriousness of eating disorders. This book provides much needed information and tools that can also augment one's treatment while educating the public."

Melissa Freizinger, PhD
Clinical Director, Laurel Hill Inn

"Cheryl's vivid and candid portrayal of life with an eating disorder, what treatment is like, and what it takes to recover are helpful to those considering treatment. She also provides insightful questions to ponder throughout the book. She generously shares her painful struggles to help others recover. Great book!"

Jacquelyn Ekern, MS, LPC
Director, Eating Disorder Hope

"Without providing triggering details (a rarity), Cheryl Kerrigan is able to share her journey of healing from an eating disorder and at the same time provide valuable, inspirational tips and tools for those who are ready to join her in "telling ED NO!" As Cheryl's story attests, "Recovery *does* happen!"

Doris Smeltzer, MA
Author, *Andrea's Voice: Silenced by Bulimia*

"In *Telling ED NO!*, Cheryl Kerrigan not only shares her personal story of her battle with an eating disorder, which consumed over twenty-two years of her life, but also about her recovery and how she managed to overcome the disorder. Included in this book are real-life exercises and tools that she used to beat ED (her eating disorder) and that can help you as well. This book shows us that recovery from an eating disorder really is possible—even after struggling with it for over twenty years. You don't have to live with your eating disorder forever. ED's chains can be broken and you can take your life back. I highly recommend this book to anyone whose life has been affected by an eating disorder. You are not a hopeless case. If Cheryl can do it, so can you!"

Andrea Roe
Eating Disorder Survivor and Author of *You Are Not Alone—The Book of Companionship for Women with Eating Disorders*, Volumes 1 and 2 (plus companion CD)
www.youarenotalonebook.com

TELLING ED NO!

*and Other Practical Tools to Conquer Your Eating Disorder
and Find Freedom*

CHERYL KERRIGAN

authorHOUSE®

AuthorHouse™
1663 Liberty Drive
Bloomington, IN 47403
www.authorhouse.com
Phone: 1-800-839-8640

First published by AuthorHouse   3/8/2010

ISBN: 978-1-4490-9246-7 (e)
ISBN: 978-1-4490-9245-0 (sc)
ISBN: 978-1-4490-9244-3 (hc)

Library of Congress Control Number: 2010902511

Printed in the United States of America
Bloomington, Indiana

This book is printed on acid-free paper.

For

Rachel

For your constant love, support, and guidance.
You never gave up on me.
I love you.

ACKNOWLEDGEMENTS

The road in writing this book has been long and winding, but the journey has been fruitful and exciting. Like my recovery, I was not alone in writing this book. I had many friends and family supporting me with every word I typed. I was fortunate to have guidance that was backed by love and friendship, and without it, this book would not be possible. I am deeply grateful for each one of you and thank you from the depths of my soul. You all have a piece of my heart.

To Rachel, my soul mate (and personal chef): Thank you for standing by me during my darkest days and helping me see the light. I know it wasn't easy at times. You gave me strength and love, and without that, I would have never been able to survive. Thank you for being patient and listening to me every single time I spoke about this book, which was often, and never turning your back. Every breath I take is a kiss from me to you. I love you with all my heart, forever.

To Dad, Mom, Peter, Stacey, Stephanie, and Stephen: You have been with me through my pain and suffering and then my rebirth of living. Thank you for your support, love, and guidance in life, my recovery, and in writing this book. Thanks for always being there every time I turned around. I love you all very much.

To Bob Bordonaro: You were there for me the day my recovery began (and still are), giving me guidance and hope. With all the falls my recovery brought, you were always there to pick me back up and help me get back on track. With tough love and kind words, you never left my side. Thank you for holding my hand on this journey; with love, I am forever grateful.

To Dr. Suzanne Gleysteen: Your wit, care, and determination in guiding me through this journey to recovery is respected and honored. I am proud to be your patient. Thank you for being there for me way back when and never losing faith in me. Your support and presence means a lot; I hold you deep in my heart.

To Thom Rutledge, the man who showed me the truth about ED and helped me realize I am separate from him, I am strong, and I don't need ED to live: From the day I met you, my heart told me you were a special man—and it was right. You challenged me, directed me, and respected me throughout my entire journey and because of that, I have found freedom. With deep gratitude, awe, and much love.

To Amy Aubertin: Thank you for teaching me to respect, trust, and love something that was once so dreaded and fearful. Thanks to you I am not afraid anymore; food is now my friend. With love and admiration.

To Dr. Daniel Mollod: Your attentiveness and care in listening to my prescription concerns brought me to a place where I could accept help in various forms and be okay with it. Thank you for guiding me and giving me the ability to feel and experience all that life has to offer. With love and respect.

To Allyson Peltier and Lauren Manoy, the best editors a girl could ever hope for: Simply amazing! You never lost sight of my vision, my story, or voice; you respected it and made it stronger. Your keen eye for detail was the icing on the cake. Thank you for your guidance, commitment, and words of encouragement.

To Danielle and James Mojonnier at Grinning Moon Creative: Thank you for taking my vision and thoughts and putting those into a design for the world to see and appreciate.

To all the folks at AuthorHouse: Thank you for your guidance (and hand holding) in making my dream a reality.

To all my reviewers: Thank you for your words of support, encouragement, and honest feedback in helping me bring life into something that once was lifeless.

To all my friends who listened to me rant day in and day out about this book and who never once told me to shut up! You always told me you were proud! I love you for that, thanks!

CONTENTS

FOREWORD

Eating disorders are complicated. And they are painful, excruciatingly painful. Eating disorders are overwhelming and often lead people into the depths of discouragement, despair, and even hopelessness.

Eating disorders are clever; they are smart. If you have an eating disorder, your eating disorder is actually smarter than you are. How strange is that? If you are struggling with an eating disorder, you know that this is true. It outsmarts you at every turn. It manipulates you with shame, praise, insults, promises, whatever it takes—whatever it takes to control your mind, your belief system, your relationships, your whole life. That is what an eating disorder will do, anything to remain in control. It never hesitates, never has a crisis of confidence and never takes a day off. An eating disorder work ethic is incomparable.

Some people will tell you that eating disorders are not about food, but that is, of course, ridiculous. Eating disorders are all about food: what to eat, what not to eat, when to eat, when not to eat, how to avoid food all together, how to eat massive amounts, how to get rid of the food that you do eat.

And some people will tell you that eating disorders are not really about your body, not really about your weight or size, or how you look in general. That too, of course, is ridiculous. How can it not be about these things when that is what your eating disorder talks to you about all day, every day?

A respected colleague of mine likes to tell her clients that "fat is not a feeling." That is, of course, ridiculous. For many, "fat" is not only a feeling, it is the feeling that defines them.

But wait…

On the other hand, eating disorders are not about food. They are about desperate attempts to be in control of something, they are about seeing yourself as different from everyone else, and not in a positive way. If you have an eating disorder, you probably suffer with relentless perfectionism, obsessions, compulsions, and what I have come to call "negative arrogance," believing yourself to be special, in that you are worse and/or more irreparable or hopeless than everyone else. "This book can probably help other people," you might think, "but probably not me."

And wait…

Eating disorders are not really about what you look like—your size or your weight. They are about feeling out of control of your own life and going to extreme measures to try to change this. They are about feeling like a freak, feeling trapped, seeing yourself as doomed to always fall short of who and what you should be.

And, of course, fat is not a feeling. Fat is a word used by people with eating disorders when they stop short of identifying the real feelings, the scary feelings below their experience of themselves as feeling fat. "I feel fat," is what you might say, instead of "I feel inadequate, ashamed, angry and deeply sad."

And, just in case you haven't noticed, eating disorders are full of paradox. They are about food, but they are not; about size and weight, but not; about feeling fat, but not really.

See what I mean? Eating disorders are complicated.

Recovery from eating disorders is simple.

I want to be crystal clear on this point: simple, but far from easy. In fact, recovery from your eating disorder may well be the hardest thing you will ever do. Recently, a client of mine who has battled both cancer and an eating disorder, told me that facing and overcoming her eating disorder has been far more difficult for her than treatment and recovery from cancer. This is what I said in response to that: wow.

Recovery is not for sissies. And there is, to my knowledge, no such thing as half-assed recovery. To overcome the control your eating disorder has over you, you must become determined and committed to do everything it will take to recover. There is no ordering recovery a la carte. No such thing as, "I'll have recovery but hold the weight gain," or "I'd like recovery with the meal plan on the side." Nope. You have to be all in.

Enter: Cheryl Kerrigan. In your hands you hold not just a book, but a box of excellent tools that, if you are willing to learn to use them, will help you to take your life back from your eating disorder. For some of you, the task may even be to take charge of your own life for the very first time. A tall order, no doubt, and that is why you need the help of people like Cheryl Kerrigan.

I will leave it for Cheryl to tell you about how and when we met. What I want you to know now, as you begin this book, is that you are in the capable hands of someone who is an inspirational leader, a compassionate teacher, and devoted advocate for you and everyone who has known the struggle and heartbreak wrought by eating disorders.

Cheryl will introduce you to my "separation metaphor," personifying your eating disorder as a unique entity that we have named "ED," the acronym for eating disorder. To quote a lyric from Jenni Schaefer's and Judy Rodman's song: "His name was Ed; he so controlled my head."[1] For Cheryl, this method of perceiving her disorder as a menacing internal force named ED, became the turning point she needed for her deepest recovery to begin. She was a quick study when it came to understanding that recovery was not going to just happen, that if she wanted recovery, she was going to have to work for it. This point cannot be emphasized enough: understanding how your eating disorder came to be, and how it controls you, will not save you. Far too often, I see people—including treatment professionals—making that mistake. There is a big difference between becoming an expert on eating disorders and becoming an expert on eating disorder recovery. With *Telling Ed NO!*, Cheryl is going to help you to become the latter.

Be sure that your pen has plenty of ink. Don't just read this book, use it. Mark in it, write notes in the margins. Keep a notebook handy, and do the exercises Cheryl describes. Really do them. If something shows even the slightest promise, then do it again, and again, and again. Cheryl is a smart woman, but that is not the main reason this book exists. The main reason this book exists is that Cheryl understands that smarts without action, theory without application, insight without follow-through, are all meaningless. Lessons from the best piano teacher do nothing to insure that I can play the piano. Recovery that stops at learning is not recovery. Recovery is about practice.

Eating disorders are complicated and painful. Recovery is simple—but hard, hard work. If you are looking for someone to show you the easy way out, you will have to look elsewhere. Cheryl will never tell you that this is easy, neither will I. But if you have hurt enough, if you are sick and tired of being controlled by this intrapersonal control freak we call "ED," then *Telling ED NO!* is your box of tools. Read on. Make notes. Discover what works best for you. Not just what makes sense, but what WORKS.

Learn from Cheryl's story; use the hell out of the excellent tools that follow; when you make a mistake, correct it; when you lose your place, find it again; when you feel like giving up, don't. When Ed tells you, as he already has, that you are not going to be able to do this, stand up, lean toward him, look him straight in the eye and tell him NO!

Thom Rutledge
February 6, 2010
Nashville, Tennessee

---

[1] *Life Without Ed*, music & lyrics by Jenni Schaefer and Judy Rodman

INTRODUCTION

I sit in a dark space, isolated from the world. I have only one companion. When I try to speak, he degrades me. When I try to run away, he catches me. When I try to be happy, he forbids it. He controls my every move. His name is ED...and he is my eating disorder.

My battle with toxic eating disorder thoughts began at age five, progressed into anorexia in my teens, and continued through my late thirties. I spent over twenty-two years as a captive of this deadly disease until I found the strength to break free.

Based on my own recovery from an eating disorder, *Telling ED NO!* brings the recovery process to life. From start to finish, this book combines over one hundred practical recovery tools with real-life scenarios and shows you it can be done. It lists various recovery tools at the end of each chapter and includes a reflection section with questions and exercises to encourage journaling and discussion that will help you navigate your path to recovery. You can read *Telling ED NO!* straight through or a section at a time to reflect on and practice the tool and exercise that each chapter holds.

From a family intervention to life in a treatment center and beyond, *Telling ED NO!* deals with my raw emotions, tough decisions, fears, and major triumphs while learning to incorporate food into my daily life in a healthy way. In writing this book, I seek not only to relate the story of my recovery, but also to bring the light of hope to others lost in the darkness of this terrible disease. Recovery is possible and it can be achieved. ED can be silenced.

From the beginning of my recovery, I viewed my eating disorder as ED based on psychotherapist Thom Rutledge's method of identifying the eating disorder as a destructive relationship (named ED) rather than a condition. I have written this book from that perspective. You will also note I refer to my eating disorder as ED from the very beginning of my life; I've done that for the sake of clarity.

From the start of my recovery I spoke and fought ED all the while, still not understanding that he was separate from me. I still felt intertwined with ED but was working through the recovery process. It was only later, through my work with Thom Rutledge, that I understood and was able to see my eating disorder as separate from me, something I did not have to identify with, something I could actually learn to defy.

For my whole life, the battle in my head was constant. ED insisted that I do everything perfectly; ED told me I was fat and ugly; and ED told me what to eat, when to eat, and why. ED had rules for me to follow in every situation. The obsessive thoughts about food, weight, calories, behaviors, and body image controlled every minute of every day. ED came with me to everything. He came with me to the playground, dance class, baton lessons, singing lessons, softball practice, color guard, school, work, and out with friends. He was always right beside me, whispering or yelling in my ear. He was my constant companion. He never let me down, or did he?

Having ED as my best friend, knowing I was never alone, made me feel safe and secure—but the destructiveness he brought with him was hurting the very core of my being. The center of my soul was slowly being dragged down into the black hole of death, and I was dying.

After many unsuccessful attempts to break free from ED, a time came when I was ready, with help, to make the commitment necessary and had the drive behind me to do it. After an intervention by my family, I began the journey to recovery from my eating disorder.

Telling ED NO! shares with you my recovery journey, during which I used over one hundred practical recovery tools to break free from ED and find freedom. In addition to these tools, I want to share with you the five main forces in my recovery process that helped guide me to freedom.

First is my treatment team—Bob Bordonaro, Thom Rutledge, Amy Aubertin, Dr. Suzanne Gleysteen, and Dr. Daniel Mollod. Professional help is essential to recovery. My team held my hand every step of the way and kicked me in the butt when I needed it. They kept me motivated and picked me up when I fell. I have felt held, supported, understood, and comforted by every one of them. Without their support and guidance, I wouldn't be here today. I trust them (which was very hard to do), and I respect and love each one of them.

The second force that helped me the most was seeing (and hearing) the separation between ED and me. It was a turning point for me—one of my "Aha!" moments. Through Thom Rutledge's intrapersonal therapy methods using exercises and role-playing, I was able to see and hear for the first time that I am not my eating disorder: ED and I *are* separate entities. It was amazing. Finally realizing that I had something to fight against rather than feeling like I was always fighting with myself was instrumental in my process of recovery. Believe me when I tell you that you are NOT your eating disorder. (I go into much more detail about Thom's work with me in Section Three).

The third force in my recovery process is the foundation on which I built my recovery: following my meal plan and nourishing myself. Without proper nutrition, your brain and body can't function properly, no matter how hard you try—and ED is always louder when you deprive yourself of nourishment. Giving your body the fuel it needs to think correctly is key. No matter how hard it was to take bite after bite, I knew I had to do it in order to continue the fight—and it worked.

Finally, the fourth and fifth vital forces in my recovery process have been patience and persistence. My treatment told me that recovery is not a straight line, and boy, is that right. I fell down and got up so many times, but most important, I learned each time. In addition, recovery doesn't happen overnight. It's a process—one that I took to heart. I had to learn to be patient yet persistent in my quest for freedom. Slowing down and taking one meal, one feeling, and one moment at a time was hard but necessary in my journey. Being persistent in *using* and *practicing* each recovery tool (sometimes repeatedly) and never giving up on myself or recovery has been proof positive.

Recovery is hard work, the hardest and most emotional work I've ever done, but it is well worth everything you go through to be free. Recovery gives you the freedom to learn, to discover, to feel, to connect, to live. Just imagine having the freedom to go out to eat and truly enjoy yourself; being free from the obsessive thoughts of calories, food, and behaviors; the freedom to exercise for the true pleasure of it; the freedom to have a social life full of friends and family. All of these things are possible.

Everyone's path to recovery is different, but patience, practice, time, and commitment are necessities for survival. Take what you can from my story, use it in your own recovery, and leave the rest behind. Remember, you have the power and ability to recover. The choice is yours. Recovery *does* happen. Never give up and always believe. You are worth it and you deserve it. If I can do it, you can do it! Believe in yourself. I do!

SECTION ONE:
WHEN ED HAD CONTROL

BORN INTO CAPTIVITY

"Unique Cheryl, you need to stay unique," ED said.

From there, a life of imprisonment began.

I came into the world two and a half months early and weighed only three pounds. The doctors didn't think I would survive, but I did. From earliest memory, my parents and everyone around me let me know I had been born a preemie and was very small for my age. I heard that message, but I wasn't the only one listening. ED heard it too.

When I was young, everyone doted on me. I loved the attention and the recognition. I felt unique and special. Unfortunately, ED took those factors and my vulnerability around them and twisted them by telling me I needed to maintain that uniqueness by doing what he said. He was beginning to lay out all the rules, and I was to obey them if I wanted to be happy, loved, and unique.

"Listen to me Cheryl, I'll tell you what you need to know. Don't worry, it will be okay," ED said.

And so it began.

"Move next to your brother so I can take a picture. Smile. You look so pretty. You are going to make so many new friends. I am so proud of you." These were all things my mom said to me on my first day of kindergarten. Sadly, I could not feel the excitement or joy she was feeling. My thoughts were quite different.

I walked around the house getting ready for my big day as thoughts went through my mind like, my feet are too big for my body, this dress makes me look puffy, everyone will be staring at me, and no one will like me. I was nervous, confused, and scared because I did not know what to expect as I began this journey called "school." My mother was telling me one thing, and ED was telling me something else. I thought, what will my day be like? Will I make friends? Will my teacher like me? Will everyone stare? Will I be alone at recess? I was being tortured by bad body image, low self-esteem, and negative thoughts. I was five years old.

Like many young girls, I took dance lessons. My mom took me to class every Saturday morning. The dance studio was right down the street from my house, so we didn't have to go far. As I walked into the building each week, my heart raced and my body temperature rose as the negative thoughts came rushing in.

As I walked onto the floor feeling exposed in my tights and leotard, I turned around and saw parents and siblings through the large window in the wall. As the music began and the teacher instructed us, the parents stared and pointed. I immediately felt they were personally attacking me. I felt like they were picking me out from the crowd and laughing at me. It made me feel so ashamed, nervous, and unloved. My head dropped, my eyes looked at the floor, and my body caved in on itself to protect my heart and soul. I wanted comfort.

Even the floor-to-ceiling mirror judged me. It told me things like "You are so uncoordinated, Cheryl. You aren't as good as the other girls, and you aren't pretty." I was confused because I liked dancing a lot, but the thoughts and feelings that came with it were so critical. I felt like I was being pulled in two directions, and I didn't know what to do or where to go.

Our dance studio had a lot of students, and at the end of the year we held a big recital at the John Hancock Building in Boston, Massachusetts. After my performance, my family took me to the back of the hall to get my picture taken. I was smiling from ear to ear because I had a fun time onstage showing the audience all my moves. I had danced in perfect harmony with the rest of my group. I needed to do it perfectly because ED expected it. I was so proud of myself. After the pictures, we went back into the hall to watch the rest of the show.

There I was, smiling with pride and being enveloped by the chair around me as my mother took out some candy bars and asked me if I wanted one. I stared into her eyes as a feeling of disgust took over my entire body. I crinkled my brow and nose and frowned as I told her, "I can't eat that, it makes you fat." My biggest decision at age six should have been whether I wanted one or both of them. I should have been able to grab that candy bar and eat the entire thing with enjoyment. But I didn't touch either one. ED had control of my words and actions and wouldn't let go. I did what he said without question.

It was Wednesday, May 12, and it was a beautiful sunny day. I was in second grade. I was laughing and playing with my friends in my backyard, and in the next instant my world was turned upside down.

The explosion came from the second floor, and glass came crashing down onto the driveway below. Flames were shooting out of the window as I began to scream. I ran into the house to get my mother. My mom, brother, and I got out of the house, ran to the end of the driveway, and pulled the firebox. Fire trucks came and neighbors gathered around as flames and water engulfed my home. I stood there shaking and crying, clinging to my mother in disbelief. Fear set in. Questions flooded my mind as my life as I knew it went up in flames: What will happen to us now? Where will we live? What will I wear? Where will I sleep?

Life continued as I lived with relatives and then eventually moved to a different city and a different school, leaving behind the only life I had known. I felt lost, alone, and afraid. My surroundings were different, and I felt uncomfortable and unsure. I had nightmares about the fire and could still smell the smoke every time I closed my eyes.

Even though my life was uprooted, I had one constant—ED. ED was my best friend, and he didn't leave my side the entire time. He told me not to worry about anything and comforted me as I began a new life somewhere else. "I'll take care of you," he said. "Don't be afraid." ED made me feel comforted and secure. He told me that if I did what he said, new friends would find me and school would be great. "You will be happy," he told me. So I listened and followed his lead. Little did I know that ED wasn't a very good friend.

Later on I took baton in grammar school and had individual, duet, and group lessons. I enjoyed the challenge of learning new tricks and getting them perfect; I always strived to do everything perfectly. I felt compelled to get every trick and every routine down without a mistake and would practice for hours to be sure I was doing it right.

During group lessons and competitions, I found myself becoming obsessed with comparing my body to others. Puberty was around the corner, and my psyche was in tune with that fact. I judged myself by what others looked like and sized myself up accordingly. Sadness set in when I felt I did not look like everyone else. I always wished I was thinner, taller, and prettier.

The competitions, which were hard enough on my self-esteem, were made even worse by the fact that they included a modeling category. We had to wear gowns and parade around like beauty queens. I never won, which reinforced my feelings of being the fattest, ugliest girl there. I tried to compensate by practicing more—which in turn made me beat myself up when I did not see the perfection ED told me I should see. I felt like a fat, ugly failure, like I would never get anything right. I felt like a loser right down to the core of my being.

Every year my baton group participated in the town's Halloween parade. My uniform consisted of a short white skirt, a short white jacket, a red leotard, and a black cummerbund. Every year I prayed I would not have to order a new skirt or cummerbund because that would mean I had gotten fatter. That fear consumed me. Alone in my room, I pulled the skirt up to my waist to see if it fit. Fear took over my body as the skirt went up my legs and hit my waist. I saw flashes of people laughing and pointing at me as I brought the clasp together to see if it would close. The next moment was crucial: Would I feel embarrassed, or would I feel relieved? ED was ready to give me direction about what to do depending on the outcome.

ED is subtle in his ways of grabbing our attention and telling us to use clothing as an easily measurable way to determine failure or success. He tells us we are successful and perfect if we fit into the mold he creates. I believed him and followed his lead. I used that skirt and cummerbund to assess my body and to determine if it was changing. If I had to move the snaps on the cummerbund to the last snap, it meant I was too fat. I always had to be sure it fit on the third snap in—the smallest. Only then would pride fill my chest and my lips turn up in a smile. It meant I had succeeded.

Reflections—Questions and Exercises:

Looking back, what are some of your earliest memories of disordered thoughts and/or behaviors? How did ED grab your attention? What age were you when it all began? Was it a gradual progression?

FOOD + MY BODY = EVIL

As it does for many adolescents, puberty brought with it intensely negative feelings about my body. But as someone who had already developed an eating disorder, these feelings were more intense and more destructive. My negative body image grew more intense, and my eating disorder behaviors became more habitual. I constantly compared myself to and competed with everything and everyone—including myself. I was aware of what everyone around me was eating and doing, and I was becoming more obsessed about calories and fat content. As usual, ED was telling me what to eat, when to eat, and how to eat, but his rules about food were becoming more involved and much stricter. His voice was more dominant and much louder. Even so, I did not want to disappoint him.

Middle school came, and my body began to change rapidly. I wanted to stay small. I felt insecure in my skin as I walked through the halls at school. I was starting to develop, and my body felt out of control. I thought, I need to make it stop, stop getting bigger, you are ruining everything. I was comparing my body to others and always wanted to be smaller and thinner than everyone else. I needed to be that way in order to be loved and stay unique. ED told me so, and I believed him. It was all I knew; it was my normal.

I was hyperaware of my body, of what was going into my mouth and how the food disfigured it (or so I thought). Now I know that I had body dysmorphic disorder, which caused me to believe that I could see my body change right before my eyes every time I ate. Every bite felt like a shard of glass going down my throat; and when it rested inside my body, it felt as heavy as cement and as big as an elephant. The disfigurement I saw in my body made me feel disgust and fear. I needed to find a way to smooth out all the fat and make it look normal again.

My friendships were being tested, and my school work was becoming more difficult. I was overwhelmed. I felt lost and alone. I was trying to figure out who I was, with which clique I wanted to align myself, what I should wear to fit in, and which activities I should do. The peer pressure was high. I felt I would be banished and alone if I chose the wrong thing. ED told me not to worry about anything. "Just listen to me and you'll be fine. I know what's best for you," he said. He told me he would take care of me and that I would be popular and smart as long as I did what he said when he said to do it. So I listened.

My low self-esteem and bad body image were rampant during this time, and I felt ugly, fat, and worthless. My behaviors grew more numerous and were intense as I tried to compensate to fix it. My younger brother was a model, and his face filled the pages of catalogs, magazines, TV commercials, and game covers. I accompanied my mother and brother on photo shoots, secretly wishing I was pretty and thin enough to partake in all the glamour. It never happened.

ED followed me everywhere. ED told me I needed to be thin to be accepted and happy. I needed to maintain that appearance in order to be loved, happy, and unique. After all, I was unique when I was born, and I had to stay that way no matter what.

Throughout my high school years, ED came with me to choir practice, singing lessons, drama, and color guard. He was beside me at every test I took and during every homework assignment I finished. I had rules to follow, and I could not disobey them. If I did, I felt like I had disappointed ED—and that was not an option. I had to prove I was good at following the rules. I wanted ED to be proud of me, to know that I was working hard. I did not want to fail.

ED told me to restrict certain foods and that certain foods were on the "bad list." Having those "bad" foods would make me a weak person and would only make me fatter. I had to stick with the "safe" foods in order to feel happy and safe. My behaviors and rituals around mealtimes were easy to hide as ED taught me how to make mealtimes look normal. The better I became at completing my behaviors and rituals, the better I felt about myself. I was a master of disguise, and no one knew or caught on; this made me feel confident in myself. I really believed that I looked and acted fine.

Time went by and things got worse. My weight continued to drop, my behaviors were dominating my life, my health was affected, my moods were up and down, and I began cutting myself to cope with daily stresses. Finally, I couldn't hide anything any longer. My parents began to comment about my weight and behaviors. My doctor caught on as my weight dropped, and I was diagnosed with anorexia in my late teens. My doctor gave me suggestions and tips to help "break the cycle" and "get back on track," but she didn't closely watch my progress—which made me think I didn't really have a problem. It gave me the permission to keep going and living the way I had been. After all, it was all I knew—it was my normal. Little did I know that ED was pulling me down a path of destruction and pain.

Reflections—Questions and Exercises:

What triggers your eating disorder and throws your behaviors into high gear? Is it emotional, physical, or social factors, or a combination of all three? What are the stressors? Write down three scenarios where you find yourself turning to ED for comfort.

PRISONER FOR LIFE?

Like most teenagers, after high school came college. I was eighteen years old and had been accepted into a business secretarial school in their one-year advanced program in Boston, Massachusetts. I was excited to get started on this next chapter of my life. I wish I could say I went alone, but ED was right beside me the entire way. He walked through the doors with me on my first day of school, and as usual, he never left my side. Because of my need to be the perfect student, feelings of stress, panic, anxiety, and fear surfaced. To compensate for these feelings, my self-injury increased and my restricting behaviors worsened. ED's rules for me were harsher, but I didn't waiver. I followed his lead.

Not only was I in an advanced program at school, I was also a member of Blessed Sacrament, a World Class Winter Guard. Winter Guard is a color guard activity performed indoors at a gym or arena during the winter months. The routines are performed to music and use various equipment (flag, rifle, saber), props, and dance moves. Spinning my rifle was a passion; I had picked up the talent in high school (thanks, Mel). We practiced three days a week and had competitions on the weekends. ED liked this because it involved a lot of exercise, and at this point in time, that behavior was becoming more dominant. I usually did my homework when I got home from practice at 11 PM. Then I was up at 5:30 AM to get ready and grab the train to school. Over and over this routine played out, and my health was declining all the while as ED had me on a short leash. He told me that if I wanted to remain strong, get good grades, and do my routines perfectly, then I needed to listen to what he said "or else"...so I listened.

ED was my go-to method for dealing with every emotion, hardship, and triumph. If I was happy, I ran and told ED. He told me, "Great job, Cheryl, but tomorrow you need to listen to me more closely and your day will be even better." If I was sad, I ran to ED and he told me, "It's okay Cheryl, I'll make you feel better. I'll fix it." No matter what feeling I had, I ran to ED for help and guidance—and he told me what to do, when to do it, and why. He was my security, so I listened. ED was embedded into my brain and had built himself into my daily life, every minute of it.

At this point I had a new doctor, and she expressed her concern. She passed along the name of a therapist to me and instructed me to make an appointment. She said she wanted me to talk about my issues with a professional in the hope that I could find a healthy way to deal with my thoughts and feelings. I went to the appointments and talked about my life and my issues, but I had difficulty admitting I had a problem. I was in denial. I didn't see the way I was living as an issue. It was just me, and that's the way it was; it was my normal.

As time went on, I got a job, got married, and built a new house. When Winter Guard ended (at that time you could only march until a certain age, and I had reached it), I took up singing in a local adult choir where I was on the board and then became the group's president. ED led me to believe that the only reason good things were happening in my life was because I was listening to what he said.

Even though things looked like they were going great on the outside, ED wore me down so much on the inside that I needed a higher level of care; my therapist encouraged a treatment facility. I was twenty-nine years old. I had to leave my post as choir president and leave my group because ED was taking over my life and winning the war against my body and brain. I was also faced with telling my boss of eleven years about my eating disorder because I had to take a leave of absence from my job. I was the company's assistant treasurer, responsible for over 150 million dollars, yet ED was taking it all from me. I thought I was in control—but in reality, ED was.

My health was compromised, my concentration was totally off, my body was giving out, and I was depressed. It was my first hospitalization in an eating disorder facility, and I was scared. I did not know what to expect nor did I want to let go of my best friend. It was what I had known for so long. I did not want to be without him.

ED was louder than ever in the hospital because he did not like the fact that I was in weight restoration mode and that I was doing what the staff said. I could not obey ED, so he beat me up inside. He told me that the staff didn't know what they were talking about and that they didn't know me like he did. He also told me that they were lying to me and only wanted me to get fat. He told me that I didn't have a problem, that I wasn't sick, and that I didn't know what I was doing. For fear of being viewed unwilling and to be the perfect patient, I participated in groups and ate according to my prescribed meal plan. I was proud of myself for going against ED, but I was not too convinced that I wanted to be without him forever. Forever is a long time.

When I was released from the hospital, I participated in the recovery process and worked hard at it. I ate according to my meal plan and went to all my outpatient appointments. I was still unsure about the process, but I was doing it anyway. Then sadness struck.

Three months after I got out of the hospital, one of my best friends suddenly passed away. I was devastated and felt lonely, sad, and angry. Rather than running to my family and friends for support, I turned to ED to help make me feel better. I wanted to feel safe and secure, held and comforted. I knew I could get that from ED. So I again participated in my negative behaviors and rituals to feel a (false) sense of control and normalcy. Well, it went from bad to worse, and I relapsed. I ended up back in the hospital. The pain of leaving work, family, and friends and learning to eat began again.

I was humiliated that I ended up back in the hospital. I felt like a failure. My family and friends seemed so disappointed. They had hoped that I was "fixed and all better" since I previously went into the hospital. They wanted to see me in good health but did not understand why it was not as simple as telling myself to "just eat." I hate those words. An eating disorder is not about food, but many people who haven't suffered with an eating disorder don't understand that.

When I was discharged from the hospital I was at a healthier weight, but my mind and thoughts were still in eating-disorder mode. I did what I was told in the hospital (and did it perfectly, I might add) but my mind, soul, and heart were not signed on just yet to living without ED. It seemed to be so much work and so much to learn, and the fear that went with it was paralyzing.

Years went by; a divorce happened, and a new life began. However, ED was my one constant. He never left my side, and no matter what I was going through, I could always count on him to be there for me. He always had a rule for me to follow, a behavior for me to do, or an instruction of some kind. What I didn't realize was that he didn't really care about me. My negative behaviors continued. My weight went up and down. My mood went up and down. I was still living life with an eating disorder. It was relentless, manipulative, and loud. It was my normal, but that didn't make it right.

At this point in my life I was happily remarried and my job was going strong. But ED always reminded me who was in control and how my life would change for the worse if I disobeyed him. I still felt like something was missing and wanted more, so I decided to go back to school at night to get my bachelor's degree. I worked full time and went to Regis College in Weston, Massachusetts at night. Another journey began. With that came more stress, more self-criticism, more perfectionism, and more rules to live by.

As usual, ED had no problem telling me what was "good" and what was "bad," what was okay to do or not to do. At age thirty-three, I became the perfect student again and would not accept anything less than As. ED was in my book bag, telling me what to eat, what not to eat, what to say, where to go, what to do, who to do it with, and why. He had rules for every situation, and I was to obey them. I was comparing myself to other adult students (and even the college-age kids on campus), and my body image was out of control.

My brain didn't shut off. I was constantly thinking about food, calories, rules, and behaviors, all while trying to concentrate on school and work. It was draining. I was still self-injuring to try to cope with it all. The more negative behaviors in which I partook, the better I felt—or so I thought. ED was in complete control. But I always felt like "I" was in control.

Years went by and I was living life with ED and going through the day-to-day motions on autopilot. I still felt unfulfilled. I couldn't understand why something was still missing because I was listening to ED and doing everything he said to do, but I still felt empty and alone. My behaviors were out of control, and my weight was at its lowest ever. My days consisted of going to work and coming home to be alone with ED. He wanted me all for himself, so I isolated myself and disengaged from friends and family. ED was my life. He dominated every moment of it, every thought. My health was failing and I was in denial. ED was my whole existence, my partner, and my life. Until one day...

Reflections—Questions and Exercises:

Is ED dominant in your life? Write down what ED is telling you right now. When and how often does ED show up throughout your day? Is he louder in the morning, at night, at work, at school, or at home?

SECTION TWO:
GAINING THE UPPER HAND

THE INTERVENTION

The nightly news was on TV as I dragged my frail, exhausted body to the kitchen sink with my dirty dinner dishes. I was at my lowest weight ever, depressed and isolated from everyone except ED. As I was cleaning off my plate, the doorbell rang. That was odd because it was a Thursday night and we were not expecting company. Dread overcame me; the thought of seeing and entertaining someone was too much for me to bear. "Oh God, who the heck is that?" I said. My spouse Rachel answered the door, and in came my brother and father. They looked so serious. Instantly, my stomach started doing flips as I became more nervous with each step they took.

"What the heck are you doing here? Is everything okay?" I asked.

"Sit down, Cheryl. We need to talk," they answered.

The smile on my face became a frown as they walked into the kitchen. There I was with all the people I love, and I had nothing but fear running through my veins. I thought, *What is happening?* It felt like my life was about to change, and I did not know if it would be for the better or the worse. I was afraid.

All the muscles in my body were tense as I took a seat at the kitchen table. The TV was turned off, and silence filled the room. They all stared at me with a look of concern.

Scary and horrible thoughts came to my mind. Panic started to set in. I thought, someone is sick and dying and they have come to break the news. Who was it? Who was sick? Was it my nephew? My niece? Who? Someone say something! I was frantic. I needed to know what was happening!

Without hesitation, they began firing away at me: "Cheryl, we love you and we are worried about you. You are very sick, and you are slowly dying. You need to get help NOW. You are withering away."

I saw their lips move and heard the words come out of their mouths, but it took me a minute to realize what was happening. This was an intervention! I thought, you've got to be kidding me! Shock, then anger enveloped my entire being. I was practically shaking at the table from all the adrenalin.

I yelled back at them, "I'm fine. You don't know what you're talking about! I'm functioning perfectly fine!"

Rachel replied, "Cheryl, you are not fine. You need help in order to get better, you need to go to treatment."

"NO, I DON'T!" I said.

My brother said, "Cheryl, your eating disorder is beginning to affect the kids, and I cannot let that happen anymore." I sat there, stunned. Did he just say I cannot see his kids unless I get help? Grief immediately overpowered me, and I began to cry. The thought of not being able to see or be with my niece and nephew was heart wrenching. My heart felt like it was being ripped out of my body and thrown onto the floor.

Rachel, my dad, and my brother didn't let me up for air. Rachel told me I needed to call the treatment center for an intake and go in to get help. ED was shouting at me all the while, telling me I was fine and they were blowing things out of proportion. ED was telling me just to sit there and listen to them, they would be out of there in no time and things would get "back to normal." But what was "normal?" Was obsessing about food and weight, behaviors, triggers, bad body image, isolation, cutting myself, and depression the "normal" I really wanted?

The intervention went on for over an hour. It was exhausting. When they were done talking and expressing their feelings, they each gave me a hug and told me they loved me. Rachel walked my dad and brother to the door as I sat motionless at the kitchen table. I could not move. I was like a statue. My body felt like I had just ran a marathon; it was overworked and needed a rest. My eyes were swollen shut from all the tears, and I was hollow and empty inside. I had no fight left in me. I had used up all my energy and was depleted. I got up from the table, shaking with emotion, and went alone into the dark living room.

I sat on the sofa with my knees bent up and my arms wrapped around them and cried, rocking back and forth and wondering what to do. I said to myself, "I can't go into treatment, I do not have time; I will lose my job; I cannot leave my family and friends." The questions and excuses were constant. ED was saying one thing, and my family was saying the complete opposite. I thought, who should I believe? What should I do? I was so confused. I went to bed that night with swollen eyes, a heavy heart, and confusion rifling around inside my head. I still had not come to a decision as I closed my eyes for the night.

I awoke the next morning with a splitting headache. My body felt like I had been hit by a truck. I was lethargic and sad as I went about my regular morning routine. A day of decision making was ahead. I was happy it was Friday but was uncertain what events would play out in the day before me. I wondered, what am I going to do?

The office was empty and quiet as I walked through the door. I sat at my desk, stared at my computer and just thought—thought about everything and everyone. Scenarios from my life flashed in my head. Thoughts about where I had been, where I wanted to go, and what I wanted to become rolled around inside my brain. I was petrified. I wanted to make the right decision but was unsure of what that was. I felt alone and confused. With a heavy heart I said out loud, "Oh God, what should I do?"

In a span of forty-five minutes, my emotions went from fear to loneliness to panic—and then it happened. It was like a flash of lighting, clarity just for one split second; I realized I didn't want to live like this anymore. My family was right. My eating disorder was killing me, and I needed help to get better. I had come to a decision. I thought to myself, I better hurry and do it before ED overpowers me and I change my mind. I got up from my desk, walked into a spare office, closed the door, and picked up the phone. My heart was beating out of my chest, and my hands were sweating so much that it was hard to hold the receiver. It took me fifteen minutes to actually dial the number because ED was trying to talk me out of calling. He told me I was not sick enough to get help. He told me I was too fat to go to treatment; "They will not accept you," he said. He told me I was fine and my family and friends did not know what they were talking about. "Everyone's blowing things out of proportion," he said. "Let's compromise, Cheryl. I'll let you gain some weight so they will get off your back and everything will be fine." I was agreeing with ED one minute, and then before I knew what was happening, I heard someone say "hello" on the other end of the phone.

My heart and mind were racing. I was stuttering. Fear prevented me from speaking a word. As I stumbled for the right words to say, I just broke down and sobbed. I told the woman on the phone, "I need help." She calmed me down and told me she was happy I called, that she would be happy to help me. We talked for a while and I felt held, safe, and warm with her words of encouragement coming through the receiver. I had made a connection. I thought, I can do this; I will be okay. I felt strong, alive, and scared all at the same time. When we hung up, I had scheduled an appointment for Monday. I thought, treatment facility, here I come!

Recovery Tool: Trust

Recovery tools within the chapter: Asking for help

Reflections—Questions and Exercises:

Trusting someone other than ED is vital to your recovery. Have any of your loved ones expressed concern for your health lately? We all need help seeing things from a healthy point of view, not ED's. Think about people in your life that you trust. Who will you trust to help you get rid of your eating disorder—a family member, a doctor, a friend? Take the first step and reach out to them.

THE TREATMENT FACILITY

I woke on Monday morning with my stomach in a knot. Even though I was covered in a fluffy down comforter and was cozy warm in my bed, thoughts of uncertainty and fear sent chills throughout my body. I thought, am I strong enough? Can I do this?

The sun was shining through my bedroom window and reflecting off my big black suitcase on the bedroom floor. I rummaged through the drawers and piled clothes into the suitcase. I was nervous and scared about not knowing what was ahead, but Rachel was there with a hug to comfort me. She told me she was proud of me.

When it was time to leave, we tossed my bag into the back of our SUV and jumped inside. As we pulled away from the house on this beautiful spring day, I turned my head to get one last look. Looking past the holly bush and through the lilacs, I could see my dogs in the window looking back at me. Sadness overcame me as I wondered when I would see them again.

As Rachel and I drove along in silence, I was cherishing our last few moments together and anticipating the events of the day ahead. After about forty minutes, we pulled up to the facility. Staff members were drinking coffee and milling around outside. The facility was stone and brick and five stories tall. In addition to the treatment facility, it held a walk-in clinic, doctors' offices, and a children's hospital. When I arrived I wondered if this would become my new home for a while. That building held the key to my new life—a life of freedom. I knew it would be tough to walk through those doors but there was a rainbow on the other side for me.

I walked in, bag in tow, and wondered which of the four programs they would admit me to, if any. As I rode the elevator up to the fourth floor, my body was shaking inside with fear. Doubt was in my mind, but hope was in my heart. My chin and lips shook with fear as I stepped off the elevator into the entryway of the locked unit. I picked up the phone on the wall and checked in with the nurse on the other end. There were a few oversized chairs and a small sofa in the waiting area. I flopped into a chair and waited patiently for them to come get me.

ED said to me "What are you, stupid? What are you doing?"

As I sat there talking with Rachel, my eyes filled with tears as the anxiety and fear engulfed me. It seemed like hours had passed, but it was really only minutes later when a nurse opened the door to say they were ready for me.

I was scared, but I entered the intake appointment with an open heart and an open mind. I had faith that whatever they told me to do would be what I needed to do to get healthy.

They brought me to the "family room," which was filled with formal end tables, a big and fluffy maroon sofa, and a large green wing chair. The window was open, and the smell of fresh air helped soothed my fear.

When the doctor came in, I instantly got nervous. I thought, what is he going to ask me? Am I going to get into the program? Will I have to eat in front of him? My thoughts were going through my head like a cyclone. He was tall with short brown hair, a beard, and glasses. When he greeted me with a soft handshake and a reassuring smile, my nerves started to settle down.

"Cheryl, how are you doing? Do you need anything?" he asked, then added, "I'm glad you're here." He seemed kind and had a calm yet confident demeanor that made me feel he would take care of me.

He sat down and began the intake. His questions came one right after another. My fear subsided as I concentrated hard on my answers to his questions. He asked what types of behaviors I had, what I consumed in a day, did I sleep through the night, did I self-injure, did I want to hurt myself, what was my family and health history, and so forth. He energetically wrote down my responses. As I sat across from him like a scared little kid who didn't knowing if she was doing good or bad, my nerves came back. In fact, they had me going so much that my leg was shook incessantly and I began to fidget.

Finally, the interview ended. I was sent to the lab for blood work and then back to the room to wait. I wondered, what will be my fate? Am I in or am I out? My mind was going crazy with questions, and I was pacing back and forth with anticipation. While I waited ED told me how stupid I was and how I didn't know what I was doing. He told me all I needed to do was to listen to him and everything would be fine. "Just walk out now and go home," ED said. The intake had lasted a total of two hours, and it was another two hours before I found out my fate. As I waited, I reflected that the process had been exhausting, and to have revealed so much was humiliating at times, but I was proud that I had pushed through it because I knew it was the only way I could begin to heal.

When the doctor came back into the room he said, "Cheryl, let's show you to your room." Tears of relief and gratitude filled my eyes. I had just been given a chance to live. At that moment I knew I was not going to die from this disorder. I had just been given hope, and I took it with open arms. I was not sure what would happen next, but I was sure about one thing: I knew I was on my way to recovery. Even though my mind was set on recovery, ED was screaming in my ear, "NO, don't do it. It won't work, only I can help you, Cheryl."

I found myself being admitted to the inpatient unit of the program. My new home was behind locked doors with twenty-four-hour care, and 100 percent of my time would be structured. I was there to get medically stable and to concentrate on myself and begin the recovery process. I was being given another chance at life, and I was going to take it.

I was in Room #3, and I had a roommate. The furnishings were minimal—two twin beds, two bedside tables, and four chairs. I began unpacking my bag with a cautious spring in my step. I had brought pictures of Rachel and my dogs and my niece and nephew, my stuffed cow Moo Moo (an anorexic who sleeps with a stuffed cow—interesting, eh?), arts-and-crafts supplies, a book, a DVD player, my iPod, and my journal. As I set them out, I was thinking about how much I was hoping to find the bigger pieces of myself, those without ED. I knew I had a tough fight ahead—and it was mine to win or lose.

I had determination in my heart and soul, but I was overwhelmed with fear. ED had no problem reminding me that I was doing everything wrong and that these people didn't know me like he did. "They can't help you like I can," he said. Being away from my home and family was tough enough, but I also faced something even more difficult, the one thing I hated most—eating.

The dining room held about twenty-five people and had three large tables, two refrigerators, a microwave, cabinets, and a sink. One side of the room was a wall of windows with a view of Boston in the distance. There were plants and flowers on the windowsill, and there were distractions all over the walls and ceiling. These included affirmations like "Believe in yourself," "You can do it," and "Stay strong." There were questions and topics taped to the wall to promote discussion and thought, and music played in the background.

I walked in carrying my tray of food and immediately felt additional anxiety because I knew I would have to eat there. ED was chatting in my ear the entire time, telling me I did not need to be here and that I was going about this all wrong. This first meal at the facility was very difficult for me, and I cried with each bite I took. I felt guilty and like I was doing something wrong by eating. My hands shook and tears filled my eyes as each piece of food passed through my lips. It was torture. The room was filled with strangers, and as I sat there, I felt as if a beacon of light was shining down on me, singling me out as "the new girl." The pain and anxiety was very intense, and my only solace was that I knew I was not the only one who was feeling this pain. I was surrounded by people just like me, and it was comforting to know that I was not alone.

I woke the next morning to another bright spring day. The sun was shining through my window as it hit my skin and warmed me all over. I stood in line for the bathroom, and I got the corner shower—the one with windows and sunlight coming through! I thought, is this a sign of things to come? I was ready for the day ahead, a day of new beginnings. Watch out ED, here I come!

Dr. P, the psychiatrist, came and got me for our first meeting. He looked to be in his late thirties or early forties. He had dark hair and spoke with a soft voice. He started the session by asking a few routine questions. Then he asked about my behaviors and thoughts. I was open and honest with my answers because I wanted recovery and knew I was in a safe place that could help me. I had made the decision and I was ready.

Dr. P told me about medication that would help calm down my racing thoughts and fight my depression. I was not one to take pills, and having to use them seemed like a failure to me. But I was at my wits' end, and I knew that I needed all the help I could get. My mind was constantly on the go and did not take a break. I obsessed about everything from the weather to food to behaviors. I never got a rest. It was exhausting to always have my mind going, going, going. I could hardly sleep at night because my mind would not stop. So after careful consideration, I made the decision to take the medication. If it could help slow down my racing thoughts, I was open to it.

Next, I moved on to a meeting with the nutritionist, Lindsey. A young woman in her late twenties or so, she had long, dark hair and a great smile. Her calming and friendly personality got me through the excruciating process of talking about meal plans. During our discussion I laid bare all my anxiety and fear, and I was often in tears as certain foods and amounts were brought into the conversation. Talking about food and meal plans was paralyzing for me, but Lindsey handled the painstaking process with kid gloves. She was able to help reduce my anxiety by listening to my fears and concerns and working with me. We had a plan in place (which ED was ticked off about), and I was confident in my ability to follow through with it.

Dr. B, the medical doctor, did the usual checkup and lab work and checked in with me about certain concerns I had regarding my health. Routine EKGs were scheduled and done right in my room. Anything I needed or worried about was taken care of for me.

Then it was time for me to meet with my social worker. I was nervous. I wondered, will I be able to open up and get what I need from this person? Will this person really be able to relate to me and understand me?

As I was finishing up a group in the group room, a man walked in and asked for me by name. I did not know who he was but followed his lead. When we were outside in the hall, he turned to me and said, "Hi, Cheryl. I'm Bob, your social worker. Let's go to your room and talk." I walked down the hall with my eyes wide and my gaze pinned to the floor. My first thoughts were, there is no way I will be able to talk to a guy. This will be totally useless. I came here for this? Why me? I was angry and disappointed. I imagined that fear would make my walls go up, and I wouldn't be able to relate to a male therapist.

Bob was tall with dark hair and wore glasses. We got to my room and closed the door behind us. He reintroduced himself to me and began to talk. I had no idea what to expect or how I would react to all of this. Despite my negative thoughts about him, I reminded myself why I was here. I listened intently to what he said. To my surprise, he made a very positive impression on me. I could tell he knew his stuff and, most important, that he understood all my craziness.

"Do you want to get better?" he asked.

"Yes, that's why I'm here," I replied.

"Tell me the types of things you are hearing in your head," he said.

I was hesitant to answer this at first for fear I would sound like a crazy idiot, but I knew I had to press on or my recovery would never work. "I am being told that I do not deserve to be here," I said. "I am being told I am not sick enough to be here. I am being told you do not know what you are talking about and that I should not trust you." I also told him about the racing thoughts I was having about calories and food.

He listened to me without judgment, and we talked about what I had said. He assured me that I was not crazy and that he understood. He was compassionate and very honest and up front. I was actually very comfortable working and talking with him. By the end of our session, I realized that I needed and really wanted him to be on my side through my recovery process. After the session, I couldn't stop thinking about it for the rest of the day. I could not believe I had actually connected with a male therapist. I was shocked!

Days came and went with one meal and snack after another. The refeeding process was uncomfortable for both my mind and my body. Food had been a foreign object to my body and it was now reintroducing itself. I had to trust the process and trust my body, which was a difficult concept to wrap my head around. Trusting my body was definitely not something I was accustomed to, but I had to start somewhere. At this point, ED was so loud, and he grew angrier each day. He was belittling me and telling me I was stupid and getting fatter.

"You don't know what you are doing, Cheryl. You are ruining everything we've worked for. You need to listen to me," ED exclaimed.

Even though ED was loud, the groups were beneficial. I was learning some new skills and tools to help interrupt my eating disorder thoughts, like thought stopping, affirmations, and distraction. The question was, would I be able to put them to use outside of this cocoon of safety? Being in the hospital was difficult and arduous, but it was also comforting because everyone around me knew how and what I was feeling at any given moment. The real world was not like this. No one in the real world can possibly understand the daily struggles people with eating disorders go through. That kind of understanding can only come from living it.

While in the hospital, I was fortunate to have friends and family visit me every single night. I was never without support. My dad came to see me every night, and he always asked how my day had been, how I had done with the food that day, and how I felt about it. And he encouraged me by telling me he loved me and by saying, "Stay strong, honey. You can do it."

Friends came to see me and we sat in my room, crowded around my bed, and chatted about the daily goings-on at home. I loved hearing about what went on at work, the latest family dramas, and their plans for the upcoming days. It helped to occupy my mind with something other than all the eating and feeling I was doing day in and day out. These visits were an invaluable support for my recovery. I knew I wasn't alone.

One of the great things about their visits was that they brought me fun arts-and-crafts projects. Distraction is a helpful way to get through a tough time. These projects gave me something to do right after meals—and that helped take my mind off the food I had just eaten. I also listened to music or read my book. It focused my energy on something other than the negative thoughts and behaviors I wanted to partake in.

The facility also provided groups for art therapy and dance therapy. This was very interesting and new to me. Through these therapies, I was forced to notice many uncomfortable feelings that were part of my eating disorder. They brought to the forefront my insecurities, self-judgment, low self-esteem, fear, and anxiety. My heart raced, my mind raced, my insides shook, and I felt exposed—like I had when I was little. But bringing those feelings to the surface and utilizing dance and art to work through them was liberating. It was interesting to use a positive behavior rather than a negative one.

The nutrition groups were key as well. These groups taught me how my body reacts to certain foods and what I needed for proper function. Learning why I need certain foods and oils in my diet and how they benefit my brain helped me when I struggled while eating them. I tried to remember there are only benefits to adding foods to my diet.

Don't get me wrong, I was a bit skeptical about all of these groups, especially because ED told me to be, but I took notes, took in the experience, and had an open mind. If your mind is closed to recovery, none of the information will seep in. Your logical mind must take over in these instances. ED was loud and obnoxious and was yelling at me the entire time; but I knew

I was taking critical steps toward recovery by participating, and that was the most important thing.

Recovery Tool: Inpatient treatment

Recovery tools within the chapter: An open mind and heart, arts and crafts, talking with friends, support groups, talk therapy, affirmations, music, journaling, reading, expressive therapy (dance and art), nutritional therapy, family, friends, following a meal plan, honesty, trust

Reflections—Questions and Exercises:

Have you ever thought about entering treatment? What's stopping you? Write down some thoughts about what may be holding you back from accepting professional help. Is ED telling you not to go? Don't believe him! Push the fear and ED aside and write down what you would hope to get out of going into treatment.

LET PEOPLE IN

While you're in treatment, you are away from your friends and family and are in a place that is difficult, uncomfortable, scary, hopeful, and exciting all at once. You are vulnerable as you put your heart and mind into the hands of people you do not know. You may ask yourself, "Am I safe? Will these people really help? Are these people nice?" For me, the answer to all these questions was yes!

It was pretty evident from the moment I walked in that the staff was there to comfort me and to help me get better. They talked to me and treated me like I was a human being, not a disease. They showed me respect and expected respect back. The staff was always at the ready and was attentive to my individual issues. They understood that all the inpatients were doing the one thing that scared us the most—eating. They did not downplay that fact and were very patient.

There were many staff members I looked forward to seeing every day to help me get through the pain I was dealing with. These individuals put a smile on my face and reminded me what I was working toward and what I was leaving behind. Caitlin, Lindsay, Kayla, Mercy, and Nadia are just a few of the staff members that held my hand on many occasions and brought a smile to my face when it was a frown. However, I do have to tip my hat to someone in particular. Janice was a staff member I connected with. Through her stories, comments, and questions, she made me realize what I was capable of and what I had to offer myself and the world around me.

Janice was there bright and early every day with a smile, a witty remark, and a look that gave me the confidence and willpower I needed to get through the day. We bantered back and forth with each other throughout the day, and she checked in with me to make sure I was doing okay. She gave me a wink or a smile and that helped me make it through. We had nicknames for each other; I called her "J" and she called me "C." She treated me with respect, and I respected her. Her presence made a difference in my recovery and allowed me to keep moving forward, and I cannot thank her enough.

Every staff member offered something to help me through the treatment process. My mind and heart were open to what they had to say and what they wanted to teach me. I took it all in and let it work for me. I was blessed to have these individuals touch my life. They each gave me something that I was able to take with me and use in my recovery. They *all* have a special place in my heart.

Recovery Tool: Let people in

Recovery tools within the chapter: An open mind and heart, honesty, trust, laughter

Reflections—Questions and Exercises:

Many people come and go throughout the recovery process, and each brings you something different and unique. Write the names of some people in your life who have helped you or who have been positive influences in your recovery. What have they given or taught you?

COMMUNICATE WITH SUPPORTS

After a lot of hard work as an inpatient in the program, I became medically stable. Then it was time for me to move on to the next phase, known as day treatment (or the partial program).

After inpatient treatment, I was released to go home on the condition that I continue day treatment. It was so nice to be home with my family and my dogs in my own surroundings. I loved waking up in my house, sipping coffee at my kitchen table while talking to Rachel, patting my dogs and watching the morning news. As nice as it was, I knew that I needed to be aware of the triggers in my environment and continue to use healthy behaviors rather than running to ED.

I showed up to the program fully rested after a good night's sleep in my own bed for the first time in a while. Day treatment ran from 8:00 AM to 2:30 PM and was on the second floor of the same building where I had been an inpatient. The layout of the space consisted of a large group room, a small waiting area with a sofa and chair, a dining area with a refrigerator, a bathroom, and a few offices.

The group room was filled with chairs, bookshelves that held games and arts and crafts, white boards, and affirmations posted all over the walls such as "You have the power," "Strength," "Fight," "Hope," "Life," "Faith," and "Peace." The only drawback was that the room didn't have any natural light. All the illumination came from overhead fluorescent lights. For me, it was tough not to have windows or natural light. It seemed a bit glum. But no one else seemed phased by it, so I let it go. I was there for a purpose and nothing would get in my way—not the lack of windows, not anything.

Our meals consisted of a morning snack, lunch, and an afternoon snack. We were responsible for following our meal plan at home for breakfast, dinner, and evening snack. We ate our morning and afternoon snack as a group in the kitchen and went to the café for lunch. We all had two choices for each snack. We followed our own individual meal plans for lunch.

It was nice to be out of the inpatient hospital setting and to be in a more relaxed environment. There were still rules that had to be followed, such as going to the bathroom in two's and no talking about behaviors, calories, weight or sizes, but they were for our own safety.

During the day we participated in groups. Some of these included dialectical behavior therapy (DBT), which is a therapy method that uses the four modules of mindfulness, interpersonal effectiveness, emotion regulation, and distress tolerance; cognitive-behavioral therapy (CBT), which is a psychotherapeutic approach that uses goal-oriented and systematic procedures; relapse prevention; nutrition; expressive therapy (art, dance); goals group; yoga; and weekend planning. Each support group brought its own dynamic into my recovery plan.

During art therapy one day we were asked to draw a bridge to recovery. At this time, there were six of us in the group. We were all in the kitchen sitting around the table. Unlike the group room, the kitchen had nice, natural light that came in through the windows. Music played softly in the background. There were art supplies on the table—paper, markers, crayons, pencils, and paint. We had no instructions other than to draw what we saw and felt.

I am not a very good artist, so my drawing was childlike, to say the least. I positioned myself at the end of the table near the window, grabbed the black, purple, yellow, and pink crayons and started to draw. At first, I drew without judging myself. But then the judging crept in. I began to judge my drawing, my feelings about the drawing, and myself; I compared my drawing to the others' drawings. I felt inadequate and became more emotional with each stroke I drew. The judging became incessant, and I started to cry. I felt like a failure. I wanted to run to ED or self-injure so I could feel better. I wanted to run out of the room, to hide and be alone. I did not want to feel the pain or the humiliation. I wanted it to go away!

Before entering the program, I would have "fixed" these feeling by running to ED or self-injury. I could not do that any more. I *chose* not to do that any more! I was forced to feel the experience and work through the pain and discomfort. And with the collective help of my fellow group members and the teacher, I did get through it.

They helped me by talking me through my thoughts and feelings and by allowing me to cry throughout the process of drawing my bridge. I used my new, healthy behaviors to push through the difficult feelings. I was able to work on not judging myself. Even though the experience was a tough one, the result was positive because I learned how to get through a feeling as it was happening without using a negative behavior. I felt my feelings, accepted them, and then moved on.

Being in day treatment brought me out of the safe inpatient "cocoon" and into real life and a daily routine. Work stresses, life stresses, and recovery stresses were all part of my daily life, and dealing with them in a new and healthier way was going to be my greatest challenge.

Fortunately, I was able to take each scenario to my peers in the program and brainstorm with them on ways to avoid eating disorder behaviors and incorporate healthy behaviors in their place. The daily support of groups and new friendships while real life played out all around me was a huge advantage in supporting my recovery.

When day treatment came to an end, I knew I would be put to the test of using the tools I had learned there in my daily life. Luckily, I had the support of my family and friends to help me during this most difficult journey, and I was ready for all the peaks and valleys that lay ahead.

Recovery Tool: Communicate with supports

Recovery tools within the chapter: Day treatment, CBT, DBT, support groups, eating with supports, expressive therapy (art), affirmations, following a meal plan, yoga, crying

Reflections—Questions and Exercises:

Self-judgment is harsh but seems to go hand in hand with ED. When and if you find that you're judging yourself, which of the following tools might you use to work through the negative thoughts: affirmations, journaling, chatting with supports, drawing? To see yourself in a positive, nonjudgmental light, write three positive statements about yourself.

MY TREATMENT TEAM

From the first moment I entered treatment, the faculty always brought the terminology and importance of a "treatment team" into play. A treatment team usually consists of a medical doctor, a nutritionist, a psychiatrist, and a therapist. When I began recovery, I did not have a treatment team in place. Sure, I had a therapist and I was seeing a doctor here and there to check my weight, but they did not exclusively deal with eating disorders. They took care of me the best they could, but I needed more, something different.

After soul searching, I realized I needed to find an outpatient treatment team that would support me in recovery and that specialized in eating disorders. It was important to me to that their backgrounds include that experience. Eating disorders are complex, and I needed people who knew all about the complexities and how to deal with them. I needed people who would fight ED with me. I needed this to save my life.

With that decision made, I decided with a heavy heart to find a new therapist as well as a new doctor. I was also on the hunt for the other two members of my team, a nutritionist and a psychiatrist. I was a bit overwhelmed by having to start from scratch, but I was determined to pick a team that would fit. Having the right treatment team is a vital element of recovery.

Research, referrals, questions, answers, frustration, and maintaining my patience became routine in my quest for a team. After some time, it all fell into place. I am a big believer in "everything happens for a reason" and getting a "sign"; throughout my recovery, that has always played out for me. Finding my treatment team was no exception. Here's how I went about finding my team.

Therapist (Massachusetts)

As I mentioned earlier, I had connected very well with my inpatient social worker, Bob. I felt at ease with him and felt I did not have to hide who I was or what I was going through because I knew he "got it." He worked with eating disorder patients every day and knew how complex the disease was. Ironically, he worked in the same treatment facility that I went to when I was first hospitalized for my eating disorder. There it was, a "sign." So when I was in treatment and still had contact with him, I decided to go out on a limb and ask Bob if he saw patients in a private practice.

I was afraid of the answer for fear I would be disappointed, but I knew I wanted him and needed him with me in this fight. I knew in my heart he was the right therapist for me, and I crossed my fingers, hoping it would work out.

I awoke that morning and decided today would be the day I would ask Bob. My insides were shaking, my stomach was flipping, and doubts were coming into my head. I lay in bed with my eyes closed and clutched Moo Moo (my stuffed cow) tightly to my chest and said, "Please God, let him say yes; I need him to help me."

The day went by, and I patiently waited for him to come get me for my session. I was anxious all day, and it was especially hard for me to eat because my stomach was in a knot. I was so nervous.

The door to the group room opened, and Bob walked in and called my name. Here it was, the moment I had been waiting for all day. I walked beside him down the hall to my room, and my heart was beating out of my chest. We walked into my room, and he closed the door and sat in the chair across from my bed. I jumped on my bed, sat cross-legged on it, and grabbed Moo Moo. I needed something to help comfort me with the fear and anxiety I was feeling.

My session started and was going okay, despite the fact that my body temperature was rising, my heart was beating out of my chest, my mouth was dry, and my head started to pound all in anticipating of my question. The session came to a close, and Bob stood up to leave. Before he got to the door, I said, "Can I ask you a question?"

He replied, "Sure, Cheryl. What is it?"

My stomach was in a knot as my mouth opened and the words came out. "Do you have a private practice, and if so, are you taking new clients?" *Oh my God, I did it, I asked him,* I thought. I sat on my bed with my eyes open wide, staring at him, my body shaking with fear as sweat was building up on my brow. I felt like I was waiting to hear if I had won the lottery.

I waited patiently for an answer, and then it happened. His mouth opened and out it came: "Yes, Cheryl, I do see patients privately. I would be happy to see you." I was elated. My insides were jumping around, I was so happy. I almost threw Moo Moo in the air in celebration. Things were starting to fall into place.

Second Therapist (Tennessee)

During my recovery I attended an eating disorder recovery workshop entitled "Divorcing ED," which proved to be pivotal. (I will talk more about this workshop in Section Three). The workshop was run by Thom Rutledge, a psychotherapist, author of *Embracing Fear*, and coauthor of *Life Without*

Ed; Jenni Schaefer, author of *Goodbye Ed, Hello Me* and *Life Without Ed*; and facilitator Julie Merryman.

The workshop was based on Thom's intrapersonal therapy model of viewing an eating disorder (ED) as a destructive relationship that you need to separate from, just like a divorce. Because I had read Jenni and Thom's book, *Life Without Ed*, I was familiar with Thom's premise and I was already identifying my eating disorder as ED.

When I met Thom at the workshop, I found him to be honest, funny, smart, clever, passionate, and an out-of-the-box therapist. I loved the way he and his brain worked, and I was intrigued by his intrapersonal therapy concept. I had never experienced anything like that before and fell in love with the way he did things. At that workshop, he made me think in ways I never had before. I felt very lucky and honored to have met and worked with him that weekend. I was amazed and truly blessed.

After the workshop, I went to Thom's Web site (www.thomrutledge. com). I knew he was intriguing and wanted to see if there was anything additional I could take away from his site to help me in my journey. While browsing around, I saw that he did phone consultations. I immediately got excited. Questions flooded my mind: Is he taking on new clients? Would he remember me? Can I really add him to my team? Does he have time for me? Can I afford it? My mind was racing. I needed to know and I wanted to know right then!

I decided to email Thom and to pose the questions I had. I sat at my desk and typed away. When I was done, I read it over and over to be sure I had said just the right words. My stomach was tight and my breath was rapid as I hit the "send" button. I was on pins and needles. I checked my inbox every hour to see if he had responded. My belly was in a knot while I wondered what he would say. What would he write back? Would he even remember who I was? Would I have another therapist to add to my team or had my luck just run out?

It seemed like forever, but a day later his response came, sitting in my inbox and waiting for me to open it. I stared at it and imagined what was inside. I took a deep breath and took the plunge. I double-clicked and, bingo, there it was. I swallowed hard and read Thom's message to me.

I was thrilled. He did remember me, he was taking on new clients, and he was going to make time for me! I sat there with a grin on my face from ear to ear, gratitude in my heart and excitement raging through my body. My hands were shaking and I could not believe it; I was lucky again. Another risk had paid off. A week later I had my first phone session with Thom (which is detailed in Section Three), and we were off and running!

Medical Doctor

Back when I was first hospitalized years ago, I was lucky enough to work with Dr. Suzanne Gleysteen (Dr. G), a medical doctor who specialized in eating disorders. She was "the" doctor in my area for eating disorders. She was dedicated, determined, and she wanted to see her patients recover. Back then I had come off the recovery path and my doctor-patient relationship with her became nonexistent. I had fallen off her radar. Could I get back on it?

I knew Dr. G was the doctor I needed and wanted, but I heard through word of mouth that she was not taking on any new patients. I decided to call the office anyway. What did I have to lose? I knew that if it was meant to be, then it would work itself out. Could I be so lucky?

There I sat in my bedroom on the side of my bed with the phone in my hand and prayed that, yet again, I would get something I needed. I placed the call and got Dr. G's administrative assistant. I told her who I was, why I was calling, and that I had been a patient years ago. She told me that Dr. G was not taking on any new patients, but she would check the records to see if I was still in the system. If I was still in the system, then I was still considered a patient.

While she was checking the database, she told me that the office purges the system every few years and that she highly doubted I would still be in there, but she was happy to look. As she looked in the computer, dread came over me. The thought of not getting Dr. G made me sick to my stomach. My eyes filled with tears as grief and anxiety set in. I needed her back. I sat on the other end of the phone and prayed for a miracle.

She came back on the line and said, "Wow, Cheryl, you're in luck. I'm surprised you are still in here." Lo and behold, my name came up; for some reason, my information had not been deleted. Tears came to my eyes as the dread turned to pure joy.

Not only was I able to become an active patient again, but I would not even have to wait too long for an appointment because someone else had cancelled an appointment while we were on the phone, and I was able to take that one.

Nutritionist

Through my research and word of mouth, I was able to find a nutritionist who also specialized in working with eating disorder patients. This was key for me because I did not want just a regular nutritionist. I wanted someone who understood the inner workings of the anorexic's mind and someone who was willing to challenge me and show me that food is my friend. That is what I got in Amy Aubertin.

I was scared to death as I went into my first session because I knew I would be talking about food, meal plans, and eating behaviors. I anticipated an anxious and emotional meeting. Even though I was extremely scared, my first meeting with Amy went very smoothly. I found Amy to be kind, smart, knowledgeable, respectful, and a gentle nudger. She was specific and detailed in her reasoning and explanations about why I needed to add and adjust certain foods, and she handled my anxiety with care. We talked about issues and came up with a plan that worked with my recovery. I was totally at ease and felt safe and secure talking with her about something that brought me so much fear.

Psychiatrist

Because I already had a therapist, my psychiatrist's role was to handle medication. Medication was a delicate subject for me, so I wanted someone who came with a reference, which is why I asked Dr. G for a name. She gave me a name and told me to tell him that I was a patient of hers. His schedule was tight, and he was only taking referrals. I gave Dr. Daniel Mollod (Dr. M) a call and set up an appointment.

At my appointment, I was impressed by how caring and attentive he was, by the way he worked and how he maneuvered his mind around what I would need to help me in the recovery process. He listened intently when I discussed my fears and concerns about my meds. He did not ignore me or push my feelings aside, and together we came up with a plan.

Dr. M listens to me about the effects of the medication and works with me to find the correct dosage and prescriptions. I trust his opinion when it comes to what he thinks may work or what might not work as well. With the addition of Dr. M, my treatment team was now complete!

Recovery Tool: Treatment team

Recovery tools within the chapter: Asking for help, taking risks, keeping outpatient appointments, honesty, persistence

Reflections—Questions and Exercises:

A treatment team is vital to your recovery. Do you have one? If not, make that first call today! When searching for your team, what questions will you ask to be sure each professional is a good fit for you? What type of experience and/or qualities will you look for in a team? What does your ideal team look like?

TELL ED NO!

It was morning and I was lying in my bed all cozy and warm underneath my down comforter with the dogs curled up beside me when I opened my eyes to begin my day. Before I could even speak a word or form a thought, I heard him: it's ED.

He spoke before I could, telling me the rules for the day. He was telling me what I can eat, what I can't eat, what behaviors I needed to do that day, what rules I needed to follow to make him proud, and how I needed to do it all perfectly or else it will mean I had failed—and according to ED, failing is not an option.

He was telling me, "Cheryl, you do not need to eat breakfast today. Actually, you have been working hard at recovery, so you can take a break and skip a few meals and snacks. A few won't matter; it will be fine, trust me."

As I lay there, my first thought was that ED telling me this meant he was my friend and was watching out for me, right? After all, he acknowledged that I was working hard and I needed a break, right? Wrong! In reality, he was being sneaky and was trying to manipulate me. If I listened to him, nothing good would come from it. I had to dig down deep and remind myself that everything ED says is a lie—all of it. I needed to fight back.

As ED was talking and giving me his line of crap, I decided to scream back at him and said out loud, "NO ED, I'M NOT LISTENING TO YOU." I had always been so diligent in listening and doing what he said, but not now. Now I wanted to leave him and live free. I wanted recovery, and I was learning to find my voice.

I said to him, "Shut up ED, I'm going to have breakfast, so leave me alone. Go away."

He spoke back and said, "You don't know what you are talking about. I know what's best. Listen to me; you don't need to eat breakfast, you had dinner last night."

I said, "NO ED, I need breakfast and I'm going to eat it. Thanks for the advice, but I'm not listening to you."

So with that exchange of words, I got up out of bed went down to the kitchen and had my breakfast. Sure, ED was talking to me the entire time, but I was talking back and telling him NO. I wanted to listen to him and not eat, but I needed to trust the process of recovery, and I knew ED was not recovery.

<u>Recovery Tool:</u> Tell ED NO

<u>Recovery tools within the chapter:</u> Following a meal plan, disobeying ED

Reflections—Questions and Exercises:

When ED talks to you and tells you things that are not productive for recovery, what might you say back to him? Find your voice and yell back. Write down five responses that you can say to ED. After you write them down, say them out loud so you can hear the power behind them. Then put your voice and those words into action. Tell ED NO.

AN OUTPATIENT CONTRACT

My first outpatient appointment with Bob was exciting. I was like a kid on Christmas morning, all smiles with excitement running through my body. I had so much to say. I could not wait to get started. Even though I was excited, ED was not; he was talking in my ear the entire time, telling me I was wasting my time and didn't need Bob. I spoke back to ED and told him to be quiet, that I knew what I was doing. I was excited to continue with this new chapter in my life—recovery—and excited that Bob was going to be beside me all the way to help guide me.

His contract was a step in this process. By signing it, I had to adhere to all the (healthy) rules and guidelines it listed. This contract helps to keep me safe and on the right path. Signing a contract like that was new to me. I was unsure of what it all meant and thought, what if I fail at it and do not hold my end of the bargain? Will I disappoint him? Nonetheless, I trusted him, so I read what he had written and signed on the dotted line. He signed right after me. It was official. I was not quite sure what to expect but was willing to go along for the ride. Here is the contract that I signed.

Treatment Contract
for Maintaining Outpatient Level of Care

1. I must maintain medical stability as determined by my medical doctor.
2. I must be able to demonstrate weight stability and progression as determined by my outpatient nutritionist and medical doctor. A minimum of XX pound(s) per month will be expected while engaging in outpatient therapy unless weight has been restored in accordance to outpatient medical doctor and nutritionist.
3. Any "significant" weight loss or continued engagement in eating disorder behaviors that place me at medical risk or when outpatient support does not reduce the eating disorder behaviors will result in a higher level of care. This will be determined by both your outpatient treatment team and treatment facility for intensive outpatient (three to five nights of structured group

program) or partial day treatment (five days per week) or inpatient treatment.

4. I must be able to ask for help or inform my outpatient therapist when feeling self-destructive, suicidal, or homicidal. I too will evaluate for any safety issues/concerns.

5. I must be compliant with scheduled outpatient appointments, follow any prescribed meal plan by nutritionist, and be open to medications recommended by my psychiatrist.

6. I will agree to have my outpatient therapist collaborate with my outpatient treatment, partner, family, and friends in an effort to support my recovery.

It was comforting to know I had this contract in place to keep me safe and on the right path. ED was really mad about that fact, but in the end Bob was there to protect me, not ED. And that is what Bob did; he protected me.

Recovery Tool: Outpatient contract

Recovery tools within the chapter: Talking back to ED, talk therapy, trust

Reflections—Questions and Exercises:

A contract is put in place to keep you safe and help keep ED away. If you don't have a contract in place, talk to your therapist about getting one. What thoughts arose for you when you were faced with a contract? What, if anything, did ED say to you? What were your feelings after you signed it?

PRESCRIPTION HELP

Most of the time, the first question anyone with an eating disorder asks when medication is brought up is, "Is weight gain a side effect?" When the doctor brought up meds with me, that was the first question I asked him. Nourishing yourself and getting healthy is hard enough, and when you add the component of a med that could cause weight gain, it becomes even scarier. I had questions: Should I take it? Will it really help me? Will it make me obese? What should I do?

I was in treatment when the subject of meds first came up, and I was scared. I thought if I took them, it meant I was a failure and weak because I couldn't get better on my own. ED agreed with me and said, "Cheryl, of course you're weak. You've completely given up the rules we lived by for so long. You don't need pills, you need me." I told ED to leave me alone and let me make up my own mind.

Even though ED was in my ear telling me not to do it, I got and read pamphlet after pamphlet on the meds Dr. P was suggesting. I wanted to get feedback from others who were taking them. What side effects did they have? Would they really help slow down the racing thoughts, as Dr. P said they would?

Not only did I want feedback, I needed to "see" if what the doctor was telling me was true. My fear about weight gain was extensive, and I needed it calmed. He told me that I would not become obese and the weight gain would be slim to none. I felt horrible about this, but I had to "see" for myself, so I asked around and found other patients that were on it. He was right. The other girls were taking it, and they were not obese. I felt like I needed proof from someone who was going through it. Just hearing it from a doctor was not good enough for me at that time. It was hard for me to trust what he was saying, but in the end I realized he would not steer me wrong. He was there to help me recover.

So after much thought, I decided to trust the doctor and take his advice and take the medication. I trusted what he told me and hoped it would help with my racing, obsessive thoughts and depression. I needed help because my mind was constantly thinking about food, behaviors, and calories. I needed it to stop and hoped the medication would help.

After a few weeks had passed, it was clear the medication was working. It was slowing down my racing and obsessive thoughts about food, calories, and weight so my recovery voice could get a word in. I was able to think more clearly. My brain didn't feel so consumed or overwhelmed. In addition, my fear of weight gain was just that—a fear. Nothing drastic happened, and I did not become obese.

Today, I am still taking my meds as prescribed and following the doctor's orders—another fear overcome on the road to recovery.

Recovery Tool: Medication

Recovery tools within the chapter: An open mind and heart, trust, talking back to ED

Reflections—Questions and Exercises:

Medications help calm the ED thoughts and fight depression, but the fear of taking them can get in the way. What fears or concerns do you have about taking medication? If you're already taking medication, what changes for the better have you noticed?

MEAL PLANNING

The thought of food brought me so much anxiety and fear that it was paralyzing. Seeing it, touching it, smelling it, preparing it, and tasting it were all things I needed to get familiar with and accept. Figuring out what to eat for each meal and snack was a struggle. Each time I tried to decide what to make for my meal, ED chimed in and talked to me the entire time, telling me what I should or shouldn't eat. It was hard to concentrate and stay focused because ED was so loud. I needed to figure out a way to lessen the anxiety, fear, and confusion around choosing and preparing my meals.

To help me with that, I decided to take my meal plan requirements and figure out meals and snacks three days ahead of time. This way I didn't have anxiety each day about what I was going to have or not have or when I would have it. I already knew ahead of time. For three days, all I had to do was look at my list, prepare the food, and eat it. I also scheduled the times that I would eat my meals and snack each day, so I was set with a plan. Knowing when I needed to eat and what I was going to eat took the anxiety out of the equation. Then I could focus on more important things, like how I was feeling.

When the three days were up, I figured out the schedule for rest of the week and added more of my "fear foods" and cravings to the meals. I knew doing this was the only way to overcome my fear and overcome ED.

Without my plan, I had too much time to think about what to do or not to do, and that is when ED would sneak in. I needed to be proactive. I didn't want him to take control, so I prepared myself and kept myself on track and safe from ED's antics.

Recovery Tool: Meal planning

Recovery tools within the chapter: Following a meal plan

Reflections—Questions and Exercises:

Sit down and make a list of some fear foods and cravings that you have. With your meal plan requirements at your side, take that list and plan out the next few days of meals and snacks. Don't include your safe foods when planning; take risks. Remember, there is no such thing as bad food. Anything goes here. Get creative and let recovery lead you.

SWALLOW UP

After each meal, my mind went into overdrive and would not let go of my bad body image. With every bite that went into my mouth, I imagined my body being morphed into a disfigured mess. I felt the food go into every part of my body and saw and felt the mess it left. It was mentally painful.

One day, while I was describing the insanity of it all, Bob said, "Let's think of it in a different way." We chatted first about the reality of what happens when the brain is starved: it doesn't think straight, it becomes more delusional, thoughts become more obsessive, ED is much louder, and it has a negative impact on your concentration and affect.

After our chat, Bob said to me, "Think of eating in this way, Cheryl: swallow up."

"Swallow up? What the heck are you talking about?" I asked.

He told me that rather than imagine the food going down into my body, I could think of the food going up into my brain. When I eat, my brain is being fed and my mind can function properly. I thought that analogy was pretty cool.

So from then on I decided to think about every bite of food going up instead of down. With each bite came clarity, and with clarity comes recovery. I was ready! In addition, thinking about swallowing up helped my body dysmorphic disorder. It helped take the edge off the visions I was tortured with each time I ate. The visions weren't so violent anymore.

Thinking about how my brain was being affected by feeding it and all the benefits of that put it into perspective and helped get my mind out of eating disorder thoughts. It was a good "reality diversion"—a diversion tactic that is rooted in reality, which gave it more power. Swallowing up is a reminder of the good you are doing for yourself, not the bad. You are nourishing your brain. When your brain is fed, you have the ability and power to fight.

Recovery Tool: Swallow up

Recovery tools within the chapter: Positive thoughts, talk therapy

Reflections—Questions and Exercises:

Feeding your brain is essential to clear thinking. When you sit and eat a meal or snack, where do you envision your food going? What feelings does it bring up for you? Fear, comfort, anxiousness, relief? What would your "reality diversion" look like?

THROW AWAY YOUR SCALE

"You want me to do what?" I exclaimed. Had I heard right? Had my entire treatment team just told me to throw away my scale? My scale? No way! Were they crazy? My lifelong friend? My scale helped me stay in control, kept me on the right path, helped guide my mood! I was dependent on it. I could never throw it away.

They kept after me every week, asking me repeatedly to get rid of my scale—and each week I refused. This went on for a while until it dawned on me that I trusted these people; they were looking out for me, they wanted me to recover. So I decided to sit down and think about what they were asking and telling me.

After thinking about it, I realized that I wasn't looking at their suggestion with a recovery mindset. And in my recovery process, I had been learning that happiness is not the number on the scale. ED and the scale weren't my friends at all! They had been ruling my entire life, and I wanted to break free. Tossing away the scale would be scary, difficult, and emotional, but it had to be done.

Tossing it away meant I would truly have to trust my treatment team to know what weight was healthy for me. It seemed unimaginable—crazy even—to go through life not knowing what I weighed. The thought of never knowing "the number" scared me to death—but I was determined to conquer my fear and anxiety.

Until then, my mindset had been that giving up the scale meant giving up control. The truth was that—scale or no scale—I never, ever had control; ED did. Sure, it was my two feet that were hitting the flat surface of the scale as the number registered up at me—but ED had complete control of every thought, movement, and emotion in response to that number. Cheryl had no say. The second my eyes read the number, ED instantly instructed me to "fix it." I was told what rules I had to follow, what behaviors I had to do, and when I needed to do them. ED called all the shots. The scale was his accomplice.

If I was going to take back control, the scale had to go. I had to learn how my mind, body, and soul functioned together at a healthy weight and not go by a number on the scale. I am more than a number!

People without eating disorders may not understand what's so difficult about throwing out a scale. So what? But when you're a prisoner of ED, the scale is your heartbeat, breath, and nourishment. It's impossible to survive without it. Throwing away my scale would be fraught with emotions. I knew I would need help. I couldn't face actually physically discarding it myself, so I asked Rachel to help me. We agreed on a date in the very near future, and that helped me feel that the decision was final. In two days, the scale would be gone for good. For the sake of accountability, I owned my decision and told my treatment team; it then became a reality.

Finally, the day arrived. I would have to say good-bye—not later, but now. I walked into the spare bathroom and shut the door behind me. I was sad. I felt like my best friend was moving away. My heart hurt. I moved the scale away from the wall and stepped on it one last time. It spoke back to me with that red digital number. Realizing that this was the last time I would ever see that number was overwhelming, and grief overpowered me. I collapsed onto the cold floor and grabbed the scale. I held it tight to my body, cradling it like a baby. I sat there naked and alone, sobbing uncontrollably. I felt like I was giving up a piece of myself. I felt like I was losing control, even though in reality I was trying to take it back.

So there we were—ED, my scale, and I. We were like the Three Musketeers! How could I be so cruel as to break us up? We needed to be together, right? The pull of these emotions was very strong. But my desire for recovery was stronger. I knew if I did not leave right then, I would be in there for hours. Most of all, I knew I needed to break the tie and say good-bye forever or I would never get well. After about fifteen minutes, I calmed myself down enough to stop crying. I kissed the scale and placed it back on the floor. I was so very sad and filled with grief, but I managed to get up and walk slowly out of the bathroom, looking back one final time.

That morning, I left the house so that that my scale could be taken away while I was out. Rachel took it for one last drive through the country, then threw it out on the side of the road where it broke into a million pieces. She gathered up the pieces and tossed them into a dumpster, never to be seen again.

I never bought another scale. I still do not own one to this day. Don't get me wrong, I'm still tempted at times to go buy a scale or to weigh myself if I come across one. However, when I feel that temptation, I keep my eye and mind on the bigger picture, which is recovery. The only place I get weighed today is at Dr. G's office, and I still step on backwards so I don't see the number. I do not let that number rule my mood or my life any longer.

Recovery Tool: Throw away your scale

Recovery tools within the chapter: Trust, positive self-talk, crying

Reflections—Questions and Exercises:

Getting rid of your scale could be an important milestone on your road to recovery. Even if you aren't quite ready yet, start the process by thinking about how you will get rid of your scale. Will you smash it with a hammer or donate it? Will you do it yourself or ask a loved one to help you? Commit to a date and toss it out. You can do it!

A SNAP ON THE WRIST

During my day I came up against thoughts of wanting to participate in one negative behavior after another. ED wanted me back and was not happy that I was committed to recovery and listening to my treatment team. He was very angry, and it was a constant battle in my head. It was tiring.

At times my thoughts put me into a trancelike state. My mind gets caught in the middle of the battle between ED and Recovery. It's hard to snap out of it and bring my mind back to the here and now. ED says, "Cheryl, I know what's best, listen to me and you will be fine, I promise." Then Recovery says, "Cheryl, listen to me, I am here to help you. You must trust me." When conversations like that happen, my head tilts and my eyes are wide and still as I just stare, concentrating on listening to the fight in my head. I need to concentrate—or do I?

I discovered that being in that trance could be a setup for disaster. I needed something to quickly snap me out of the trance. The longer I was in it, the greater the chance that I would participate in a negative behavior versus a healthy one. So I decided to work off the word "snap" and put it to literal use. I took a rubber band and put it around my wrist like a bracelet. Having it there didn't look funny or draw attention to me in any way, so I was comfortable with it. I decided that when a negative thought came to mind and I began to be pulled down that road, I would snap the rubber band against my wrist to "snap" me back into reality so I could think clearly and choose correctly—which means choosing recovery. (Don't snap to induce pain or punishment, just snap to grab back your own attention.)

So I tried it. After wearing this band a few days and practicing the technique, it was perfectly clear that it did the job of helping me snap out of the battle in my head. By snapping it, it gave me just enough of a jolt that my eyes flickered, my head lifted up, and my mind returned to the here and now. It gave me a sense of clarity so I could make a decision that supported recovery.

Recovery Tool: Snap a rubber band on wrist

Recovery tools within the chapter: N/A

Reflections—Questions and Exercises:

During the day do you find yourself in a trance while listening to ED and Recovery fight for you? Wear a rubber band around your wrist and snap it when you find yourself in a trance. List three positive steps you can take to snap you back to the reality of here and now so you can make the healthy choice.

PROS AND CONS LIST: ED VERSUS RECOVERY

During one of my sessions with Bob, he suggested doing a pros and cons list to see what ED and Recovery had to offer. Then I could make a decision about what to do based on the information I had. He said he was confident the outcome would be Recovery.

So to help myself stay focused on recovery, I sat down one day with paper and pen in hand and made a pro and con list: ED versus Recovery. I made two columns. In one column I wrote down the things ED gave me (loneliness, lies, isolation, bad body image, depression, manipulation, judgment, rules, a false sense of security), and in another column I wrote down the things Recovery could give me (freedom, strength, energy, dreams, self-acceptance, life, choices, confidence, the love of food).

It was hard to get started, but after I got going it just flowed. I was amazed. I saw that Recovery held many more positive things than ED did. ED gave me nothing positive. It was a powerful visual. I kept that list handy and referred to it and added to it often. It was a visual reality that I could see and experience.

<u>Recovery Tool:</u> Pros and cons list—ED versus Recovery

<u>Recovery tools within the chapter:</u> Talk therapy

Reflections—Questions and Exercises:

To help you visualize what ED and Recovery give to you, arm yourself with paper and pen and sit down and write out your pros and cons list. Put ED on one side and Recovery on the other. Write out what each gives you; be honest and open. You will soon see the power and life that Recovery can offer. It is much better than the one ED gives you.

PATIENCE

While in recovery, "aren't you better yet" was a feeling, a wish, and a hope that exuded from my family and friends (and even myself). People knew I had gone into treatment and they saw me eating, so they figured I was totally cured. As we know, an eating disorder is not about the food and recovery is not as simple as "just eat."

My friends and family wanted me to be immediately free of the pain they knew I was feeling. I was grateful for that but feeling that expectation/wish of being "all better already" brought me added anxiety and pressure. I felt I was expected to make a miraculous recovery and that everyone expected to see me eat, to see zero behaviors and zero anxiety, and that I would be in a good mood forever. That simply wasn't the case. It's not that quick or simple.

One day I was feeling lots of emotion. I was stressed out and anxious about an upcoming event I needed to attend. I was still learning to deal with emotions rather than react negatively to them. As Rachel and I ate dinner, she noticed that I was exhibiting some old unhealthy rituals. She calmly brought my behavior to my attention and asked if I wanted to talk; I said no. After a few more minutes she noticed I was still having trouble and asked again. I realized I needed to reach out, so I accepted her offer this time and we spoke about my feelings. I was frustrated that I was having trouble but had to remember that patience is key. Like Rachel was being patient with me, I had to be patient with the recovery process. It doesn't happen overnight.

Recovery is a process with many twists and turns and hills and valleys, and we must realize that we are not fixed lickety-split just because we are "in recovery" (or went to treatment). It can be hard for others to realize that there is no quick fix. Sometimes it can even be hard for us to realize that too. We want it to happen overnight so we can be free, but in reality it takes time. Recovery is a process. We must go through it one step at a time, knowing we may take steps back before we take another step forward. All steps, no matter if they're forward or back, are still steps; you still learn.

Recovery takes time, patience, commitment, and hard work. Having the support of friends, family, and a treatment team behind you is a great foundation of strength to upon which to build. Everything comes in time; be patient.

Recovery Tool: Patience

Recovery tools within the chapter: Talking with supports, eating with supports, following a meal plan

Reflections—Questions and Exercises:

Recovery is a process that takes time, hard work, and patience. Think about the last few days. Have you allowed yourself to slow down, experience, and feel each step of your process, or are you rushing through it? Take a few deep breaths and speak a mantra for support and grounding. Example: Recovery is a process, one that I accept with patience and love. Write down three things that you have learned over the last week about yourself or your recovery process.

HOLD ICE

My stress level was high at the office and I was on edge. During this time, ED was loud and I was having difficulty getting him to shut up so I was even more frustrated, anxious, and vulnerable. One day Rachel and I got into a fight over something stupid. We ended up parting ways, one upstairs and one downstairs. I was angry and hurt, and ED took that opening and ran with it.

ED said, "Cheryl, I know what would make you feel better. If you just cut yourself a little, you'll be able to make the pain go away."

One minute I was sitting on the sofa in the family room, and the next minute I was up and listening to ED. It was so fast and so automatic. There I was, starting to hurting myself when Recovery stepped in and said, "STOP, don't listen to him!" It was like someone slapped me across the face. I was jarred awake. My eyes blinked fast and I came out of the automatic daze I was in. I immediately realized what I was doing and stopped.

ED yelled back, "Cheryl, this will make you feel better. Trust me, I know you and know what you need right now."

I had to really think about my next action: What could I do to help with this anxiety and anger? I needed to NOT listen to ED and listen to Recovery. Hurting myself was not going to help me through my feelings, but my mind was racing and I didn't know what to do.

A step toward recovery happened next. I took my power back, and I ran to the freezer. I grabbed two ice cubes and held one in each hand. I squeezed tightly, took deep breaths and said over and over, "ED is wrong, Recovery is right." After a few minutes, I felt the cold in my hands and concentrated on that. I heard the voices in my head slow down, and then I slowly realized my anxiety and anger was dissipating.

After a few minutes I dried off my hands, took a deep breath, and realized that even though I had listened to ED in the beginning, I had stepped in and changed the behavior. I had faced the feelings and got through them. I did it. I made it through. I did not let ED keep the power. I took it back.

Recovery Tool: Hold ice

Recovery tools within the chapter: Deep breathing, positive mantra

Reflections—Questions and Exercises:

Stressful situations are part of life, and we need healthy behaviors to help us through them so we don't follow ED. When you are faced with stressful situations and feelings and ED is talking to you, do you go on autopilot? Redirect your thoughts. Listen closely for Recovery; it is there. What is it saying to you? Write down three messages that Recovery says to you when you go on autopilot.

SIT ON YOUR HANDS

I was told early on that recovery is not a straight line and recovery has its ups and downs. I heard what others were saying but until you are living it, the reality of it doesn't sink in. I did not realize how true that statement really was. You have to fall down in order to know how to get back up, and falling down does not mean you have failed.

I fell, and I needed help getting back up.

I was making progress, but ED was in my way more than I wanted him to be at this point. My food choices were becoming less risky, I was skipping meals and snacks, and I was starting to isolate again. I was scared. I was seeing my treatment team regularly, but we collectively felt that I needed a bit more help to break the cycle and continue to move forward. After talking it over with Rachel and my entire treatment team, I decided to enter treatment again to gain even more strength and knowledge than I had the last time.

Admitting I needed more help was very hard for me to do. I was embarrassed and humiliated. My first thought was that I had failed. How could I have let this happen? I had to remember that ED is strong and it takes hard work to fight him off. I just needed more armor. After I thought about it, I realized asking for help shows strength, not weakness. I wanted to get stronger, and asking for help would get me there.

Bob made the arrangements for me to go in for another intake. This time I knew what to expect in terms of the protocols, and I continued to have an open mind toward recovery. I showed up for the intake with hope in my heart, praying they had room for me.

After the intake and the waiting, they came and told me I would be staying. A big sigh of relief came over me. I was happy that I would get the help I had asked for. I had asked and was not disappointed. That was huge for me to see and feel. Knowing I could take the risk to ask for something I needed and get it brought me comfort. Another risk had paid off, and I was thankful.

I was admitted to inpatient treatment again. Even though I was not as medically compromised as before, I needed help breaking the cycle of negative behaviors and thoughts, and being in twenty-four-hour care was the way to help me with that. After getting over the initial embarrassment of being in treatment yet again, it was comforting to be around the staff that had previously helped me. They remembered me, so that calmed me down right away. Comfort and a sense of security set in, and soon we were all laughing and joking together. Their humor—and more important, their treating and talking to me like a person rather than an eating disorder—helped me push through the difficult times.

Deep down I knew I needed more help. But I was still fighting with the eating disorder thoughts, and they were getting me down. ED was trying to convince me I did not have an eating disorder. He told me I did not need anyone, only him. I fought those thoughts through positive self-talk. I told myself, I am worth it and I am brave. I am in recovery and I will get there. I also talked back to ED and told him to leave me alone. I told him he didn't know what he was talking about and I wasn't going to listen to him.

It was hard to fight through the depression and the doubt I had at times, but I had to remember the ultimate goal—recovery—and that being recovered was what I wanted. I needed to keep fighting, no matter how difficult and painful it was. As Bob says, I needed to "trust the process."

At this point, my body checking was becoming more frequent. I was using my hands to feel the parts of me that I thought were getting bigger. I needed to decrease the frequency of that behavior; I knew it would only hinder my progress if I didn't. At one of my sessions, I told Bob that I needed help with body checking. He brainstormed with me and gave me suggestions for ways to decrease the behavior and lower my anxiety about it.

Because I could body check anywhere, I needed to find many different tools to help me out in various scenarios. After chatting about it, these are the tools we came up with: sitting on my hands, sitting certain ways that are comfortable, counting to fifty, journaling, putting an object in my hands, and speaking a positive mantra. I utilized any tool that I could to stop the negative behavior. When I caught myself body checking, I used many of these tools to help me stop the behavior. It took practice, but it did work. Sitting on my hands was the tool I used the most because I could do that anywhere, and sitting on my hands stopped me from squeezing what I saw as too much fat on various parts of my body.

My mood was up and down. I had good days and bad days. I wanted recovery one moment and wanted ED the next. I wondered, was I still up for the fight? Where would recovery take me next?

Recovery Tool: Sit on your hands

Recovery tools within the chapter: Asking for what you need, inpatient treatment, talking back to ED, talk therapy, laughter, positive self-talk, counting to fifty, sitting comfortably, holding an object, positive mantras

Reflections—Questions and Exercises:

Falling down and getting back up is part of the recovery journey. While on your path, have you fallen? What would standing up and moving forward look like for you? A treatment facility, more outpatient therapy appointments, or a support group?

ACCOUNTABILITY

At the end of my inpatient stay, the time came in my recovery journey when I needed to move on to the next phase of treatment. The next phase for me would be residential treatment. At first I was not happy about it at all. I was actually frustrated and very angry. I wanted to go home and live my life. I felt like my life was on hold, and I wanted it to begin. What I did not realize was that my life had already begun—learning to live life without my eating disorder. Residential treatment would continue to help me with that.

Bob brought me over to the residential treatment facility across the street from the hospital to check the place out. As we walked over, my stomach was in a knot and my mind was all over the place with questions and concerns: Does it really look like a place I would live? Would I get along with the other girls? Do I really want to do this?

When I first walked in I was comforted by seeing the place was "normal" looking. The facility consisted of two apartments with four girls in each. The apartments were right next to each other. Each apartment had two bedrooms with a private bath in each, a living room, an eating area, and a kitchen. There was staff on duty twenty-four hours a day. The apartments were comfortable, clean, and modern. They had sofas, TVs, DVD players, and there were two computers with Internet access for us to use. The apartments had all the comforts of home.

I met a few of the counselors and saw a couple of the other girls. I was so scared. I felt like I was walking on eggshells. Everyone was staring at me and feelings of insecurity, loneliness, and exposure came to the surface. I felt like a puppy being thrown into a new home away from her mother. It was so different than being in the bubble of inpatient. I asked myself, will I be able to find the security in this phase that I have found in previous phases?

The day came for me to transition to residential treatment. My things were all packed up in bags, sitting on a dolly and waiting to be wheeled to the next new place. I sat alone in my room on the bed and waited for someone to come get me. Doubt and fear filled my body. My mind and heart were racing as I wondered, can I do this? Am I ready? Why can't I go home?

My transition to residential treatment was difficult. Bob came to see me off and wish me well, and all I could do was cry to him. I said, "Why can't I go home? Why are you doing this to me?"

He said, "Residential treatment is the next best step for you. You will do great. You are ready."

I didn't understand why I couldn't just go home. I wanted to sleep at home, cook at home, and live at home. I did not want to live in the residential treatment apartment. He assured me that "resie" (our nickname for residential treatment) was my next best step toward recovery. I needed to figure out how to incorporate certain daily routines into my life without ED. He restated his famous mantra: Trust the process. I was feeling all sorts of anxiety, and I wanted to scream back, "Take your process and stick it," but I sat there with my mouth shut and my mind and heart open to what he had to say.

As I calmed myself down, the head of the program knocked on my door. "You ready?" she asked.

I said, "No, but I'm willing to try."

I got behind the dolly and began to wheel life as I knew it down the hall to the doors that led to the outside. I turned back and saw all my friends staring and waving at me. They said, "You'll do great," and "Keep up the good work," and "We'll miss you." As I waved back and opened the door, tears of sadness and anxiety filled my eyes. The door shut behind me, and they were gone.

As we walked over to resie, words of encouragement were being thrown my way by the program leader. I was appreciative but still cautious. And then we arrived. As I walked through the door my heart was in my throat. I wondered, will I fit in? Right as I walked in, I was greeted by four girls. I was happy to see two people I knew from inpatient, one of whom was my old roommate. That put me at ease right away. It gave me strength; if they were doing it, then so could I.

My first night at resie was a little scary. I was afraid of sleeping somewhere new and was anticipating all the new things to remember and do. However, the girls helped me get comfortable with the surroundings and told me about the rules, the groups, and the goings-on. They helped me out, and I started to get excited to see what life at resie would be like.

I woke the next morning to a hot summer day. My pictures of my family stared back at me from my bureau. I went to the kitchen, grabbed a cup of coffee, sat on the sofa, and watched the morning news—just like I would do at home. I was comfortable and relaxed.

My first full day at resie was ahead, and I was brought up against a scary situation—going out to lunch. Resie was all about learning to live life without an eating disorder and how to deal with life situations as they arise. Going out to eat is a normal thing that people do. I was anxious about it but decided to use this to *my* advantage, not ED's. I decided to show ED who is boss and order something *I* wanted, not what he told me to get. To own my decision and be accountable, I told it to a few group members. Telling someone my decision and being accountable gives ED less power and gives me and my recovery more strength.

Armed with Holly the counselor and Roberta the nutritionist, our collective group walked down the street to the restaurant for lunch. We were seated at a large table in the corner. We were away from the crowd, which was good because we all needed to chat about our meal plans and get advice and help on what and how to order.

Sitting there with the menu in front of me was anxiety provoking. My hands were sweating, my leg was shaking up and down, and my heart was racing. ED was telling me to order my safe, lower-calorie foods, but I had another agenda—*my* agenda. I told him to leave me alone and said, "ED, I know what I'm doing, I don't need your help. You don't even know what I like, anyway!" I needed to stay strong and keep to my decision.

The waitress came to the table and said, "What can I get you?" My heart was in my throat as I told her, "I'll have a buffalo chicken wrap sandwich, please." It was difficult, but I stuck to my word and got what *I* wanted. After my order was out of my mouth, I felt empowered. I had pushed through the fear and won. My order even came with fries—and I ate some, too!

Throughout the meal we all chatted about our families, our work, and our struggles with ED. We were just a bunch of friends out to lunch. To look at us, you would never know how hard it was for us to do what we did. But we did it; we survived.

After lunch, we got up from the table and headed back to resie. We were proud of ourselves for accomplishing something that was so scary. We had proved to ourselves that we could do it.

Nutrition, relapse prevention, yoga, writing, and goals were just some of the groups that were incorporated throughout our days at resie. We went on planned outings such as shopping, pottery painting, movies, and bowling so we could incorporate regular fun activities into our new world of healthy living. Daily twenty-minute walks, one after breakfast and one after dinner, were also part of our days. In addition, working on the exercises from the Web site www.myselfhelp.com was part of the recovery curriculum.

Mealtimes were done in shifts because the kitchen couldn't hold eight women preparing eight different meals all at once. We had two shifts for each meal. We were responsible for planning, preparing, and cooking our own meals. We ordered groceries through a delivery service and could add anything we needed or wanted to the list (as long as it wasn't diet food).

We were also responsible for our own messes. Chores like vacuuming, emptying the dishwasher, putting groceries away, and so on were split between the groups on a weekly basis. We all took turns and pitched in to take care of the place we called home.

Visiting hours were every night after dinner from 6 PM to 8 PM. Family and friends came to the apartments to visit. We could also walk around the grounds with them. Unless we had a pass, we were not allowed to leave during the week.

Every weekend we had a four-hour pass during which we could leave the grounds if we chose. We could go home, go shopping, go to an appointment, or just stay around the apartment and vegetate. We could basically do what we wanted as long as we stayed within the program's rules, like no going to the gym or participating in negative behaviors.

I always went home on the weekends to see Rachel and the dogs. When I went home, I watched TV with Rachel, did housework, and took naps in my own bed. It was nice to feel like I was getting things accomplished and spending quality time with my family.

Being in residential treatment taught me how to think outside the box when it came to preparing meals. Learning to portion correctly and becoming more comfortable actually seeing and working with food was very helpful. Preparing a grocery list and a meal plan helped to lower my anxiety. Being in residential treatment helped to boost my confidence and most importantly, it helped me see that I could incorporate food into my daily life.

Recovery Tool: Accountability

Recovery tools within the chapter: Residential treatment, an open mind and heart, talking with friends and family, going out to eat, talking back to ED, trust, support groups, yoga, eating with supports, recovery Web sites, following a meal plan, twenty-minute walks after meals

Reflections—Questions and Exercises:

We strive to incorporate food into our daily lives. Make a list of some of your fear foods. At your next meal and snack, show ED you mean business by incorporating a fear food or two. Be accountable for it and tell someone your plan. Eating and doing what *you* want and not what ED wants will get him further and further away from you. You CAN do it!

A LETTER TO YOURSELF

Besides going out to lunch, my first full day in residential treatment brought another challenge. Holly, the counselor, told us to bring paper and a pen to group. I was new to resie and excited to see what all the different groups were about. I armed myself with the tools and wondered what group would bring. The eight of us sat in the living room and listened to Holly tell us that today's group was a writing group.

We were instructed to write a letter to ourselves about the positive aspects of recovery and about where are right now and where we wanted to go. We were going to put it in a self-addressed envelope and seal it up. The interesting part about this exercise was that the staff was going to mail our letters to us six months later. I thought that was a cool twist.

I sat in the corner of the couch, staring out the window at the tree across the street and wondering what I wanted to say to myself. I wanted to be poignant and honest. The room was quiet as we all strategically placed ourselves around the room to give everyone privacy.

I took a deep breath and began. I wrote about what I accomplished, what that I wanted from life, and affirmations that caught my eye. I wrote with passion and honesty. I didn't hold back. When I was finished, I sealed the envelope and passed it to Holly. I didn't think about it again until the day it arrived in my mailbox.

It was a Saturday, and I was having a particularly hard day. Holiday and work stresses dominated. ED was annoying me, and I was trying to stay strong. I pulled into the driveway after running errands and saw the mailman ahead. I parked the car and went to the mailbox. While walking back to the house, I flipped through the pile of mail and noticed an envelope addressed to me. At first I was confused because I knew the writing on the envelope was mine, but I had no idea what the heck it was. It was not until I opened it and began to read the letter to myself that I remembered. This is what it said:

Dear Self:
I am sitting in the living room of residential and it's Thursday, my first full day here. I was overwhelmed when I got here yesterday and was crying and scared. I settled in and am making myself feel at home. It was a bit challenging to make dinner and breakfast for myself, but it worked

out nicely. Today we went to the restaurant for lunch and I ordered what I wanted, not what ED wanted. It was hard to do, but I did order my buffalo chicken wrap. It was good. I also ate fries too. I had a great lunch.

I'm here at resie trying to get my life back. Learning how to fit food and feelings into my day, to be strong and to be "normal." I am here struggling with my eating disorder and my behaviors because I want to let go of ED's control. I want to win this battle like never before. I am building a strong foundation here with this phase of treatment and recovery. Real life is next and I want to be a part of it and enjoy each moment, for each moment is a gift.

I am really learning how to live my life without the eating disorder. From the moment I open my eyes in the morning to when I shut them at night, it is a challenge to keep things real, to learn and to feel—and most important, to eat. Despite the guilt I have for leaving my family and work again, this treatment will show me how great life is. I want to enjoy my family, my friends, my work—my life. I do not want ED to take any of that away again. I want to rise up and be free. I just wish there was a magic pill because it is very hard to overcome, but I believe and trust my treatment team. I want to be one of their patients who has recovered. I really do love life and want to be a part of it. I want to experience all the good and bad with feelings, to feel it rather than be numb to it. I want the gift of life for myself. Stay strong and always believe!

Love, Me

xoxoxoxo

Getting that letter on that day was the boost I needed to help me through the day. It reminded me what I was working toward and what I wanted to leave behind. It reminded me that I am strong and I can do it. It arrived exactly when it was supposed to.

Recovery Tool: Write a letter to yourself

Recovery tools within the chapter: Honesty, residential treatment, support group

Reflections—Questions and Exercises:

Getting a boost at just the right time during your recovery process is a nice treat. It can happen when you least expect it. To use the recovery tool, sit down in a quiet place and write a positive letter to yourself. Write about where you are, where you want to go, and what you want. Seal it up and give it to someone you trust. Tell them to mail it to you after a certain amount of time. When you receive it, you may be surprised by how much it helps. I am sure it will arrive exactly when it should.

CONNECT WITH SUPPORTS

After residential treatment it was important to me to stay in touch with the friends I had made. I wanted to stay on the recovery path and needed to continue to seek out ways to make that happen. I needed the connections, people who would listen.

Upon leaving treatment, a lot of us swapped numbers. I used those connections to aid me in my daily struggles. They knew how hard recovery was but could also envision the prize at the end. It helped to know that someone on the other end of the phone knew what I was talking about and knew how I was feeling. We brainstormed and cried with each other and met for coffee and hung out.

One day I was finding it difficult to keep to my meal plan. It had just been adjusted, and I was overwhelmed. ED was telling me I didn't need the new meal plan, but I knew better. I called a friend to help me out. I was able to tell her I was feeling scared and overwhelmed, and she was able to relate and comfort me. She knew what I was going through, and that helped me not feel so alone. We ate a snack together over the phone, and that helped me push ED aside and stick to my plan.

I also utilized my family and other friends. If I was having a hard time or having negative thoughts, I emailed someone or picked up the phone to reach out to get the words of encouragement I needed to keep moving forward. It was nice to have someone there who could redirect my negative thoughts to positive ones and give me a reality check. It was important for me to hear someone say, "I believe in you, I am proud of you, and you aren't alone."

In addition to making phone calls and sending emails, I attended a monthly recovery support group. This group featured a recovered person who told his or her story, and then there was a question and answer portion. It was great to hear his or her story and hear what had worked for each of them. I was able to take away ideas from their stories and use them in my recovery. It was also nice to see someone who had recovered standing right in front of me. It gave me confirmation that recovery is possible and it can be done. It gave me an added boost. Plus, I was able to connect with friends I met in treatment and meet new ones at those meetings. We were all supportive of each other and our quest to live life without ED. Connections with supports are important. Laughing and crying with them is much healthier than doing it with ED.

Recovery Tool: Connect with supports

Recovery tools within the chapter: Support groups, socializing, crying, laughter, following a meal plan, eat with supports

Reflections—Questions and Exercises:

Having support is an essential piece of the recovery process. You can't do this alone. When you are having a hard time, who or what do you laugh, cry, and connect with? Write down a list of supports that aid you in your recovery. How do they help you? Where can you find more support?

A SEPARATION CONTRACT

In my spare time, I volunteer for a local hospice. I keep the patients company, run errands for them, talk to them, provide comfort when they need it, and help them through difficult times. When a person is in hospice they are treated with respect and honor as they go into the next phase of their life.

I decided to put my own spin on my hospice work and relate it to my recovery from ED. I decided to put ED in hospice and write a contract for him. I figured this would help me in trying to separate from him and would help in the process of saying good-bye. By having this contract, I wanted to show ED that I mean business and wanted him gone, but at the same time I felt I needed to show him respect for all the time we had spent together and all we had been through.

I sat down at my kitchen table with music playing softly in the background. Feelings of extreme guilt came up as I wrote down words that would translate into ED moving into the next phase of his life—his death. Even though I wanted him gone, I still felt like I was doing something wrong. Nonetheless, I continued writing.

After an hour or so it was completed. ED was to transition into hospice, and I was the one who was putting him there. I was cautious but proud that had I taken another stand for myself, my life, and my recovery. Here is what I came up with.

Hospice Referral Contract

Patient Name: ED
Patient Address: Cheryl's Body and Soul
Patient Diagnosis: Terminal Disorder

This document will serve as a referral contract for the patient named above to be admitted into Life's a Journey Hospice. Life's a Journey Hospice is a well-respected hospice that offers patients comprehensive medical, social, nutritional, and spiritual care.

ED will be living out the remainder of his life in familiar surroundings. Nonetheless, changing ways, an open mind, and a new outlook will be expected. The staff of Life's a Journey Hospice—Bob, Suzanne, Amy, Daniel, and Cheryl—will show ED how to depart with dignity, comfort, and peace.

They will allow him the freedom to express himself while guiding him through the new boundaries of and around death.

Respect will be shown and given by all parties, and the stages of dying will be acknowledged and dealt with as they appear. The patient will have weekly check-ins to assess his progress, and he will be given the help needed to see him through this difficult transition. At the end of three months, the patient will be reassessed and modifications, if needed, will be made to his treatment plan for future care.

The staff at Life's a Journey Hospice is committed to ED in the quest for end-of-life care.

—Signed by me and my entire treatment team

I gave a copy to Bob and kept a copy for myself. Having it in writing that I acknowledged and respected ED but needed to say good-bye to him was empowering and sad at the same time. This contract was twofold. Not only did it help prepare me to live without ED, it also prepared ED to live without me.

Recovery Tool: A separation contract

Recovery tools within the chapter: Writing, music

Reflections—Questions and Exercises:

Saying good-bye to ED is difficult but is necessary for your survival. How would your separation contract read? What would you include? Sit down in a quiet place and write a separation contract between you and ED. Authenticate it with your signature, and have your treatment team sign it. Make it official!

TANGIBLE OBJECTS

As I moved away from ED, the feeling of loneliness was very strong. I was losing my best friend and felt sad and alone. Even though I had my treatment team, family, and friends, the void was heart wrenching. The grief was overwhelming, and there was a hole inside my heart.

The voice of Recovery was still present but weak at times when the feeling of loneliness enveloped it. I listened closely, and I knew it was there. Deep down inside my soul, I knew I was not alone. I realized I needed something to fill the void inside, to give me strength and help me feel loved and connected. My dogs helped me with their unconditional love, and they were there in an instant with a wag of their tails and kisses. However, I needed a tangible object, something to hold tight to my body when I felt sad and lonely.

I ventured out to the mall one Saturday morning with a mission: find something that spoke to me, something that made my heart warm and made me feel held and safe. I went from store to store but found nothing. ED talked to me as I was wandering about. He said, "Why are you leaving me, Cheryl? I'm your best friend. You can't replace me. Come back to me and you won't feel alone."

I was feeling guilty and defeated when Recovery said, "Don't give up Cheryl. Keep looking. ED is not your friend. You can do this." So onward I went.

I walked into the next store and browsed around. They had figurines, magnets, cards, candles, and toys. I walked into the kids' section and looked around to scope the place out. My gaze landed on a section with stuffed animals in it. I walked over to take a look.

There I stood, still as a statue as my eyes wandered over a sea of plush. I began to feel excited; something inside me was shifting. I thought, I'm in the right place. I began to move the stuffed animals around, picking them up and looking into their eyes to see what I felt. There were dogs, cats, lambs, bunnies, and many more. I was not prejudiced as to what I was looking for; I just wanted the "right" one. I wanted the animal to speak to me, to tell me "I'm the one, pick me, I'll help you."

I stood back from the rack and looked from afar. Then I saw it. It was looking right in my eye and telling me "I'm here, I'm here." On the top shelf, peering out behind a gray bunny, was an orange giraffe. Our eyes met and I instantly knew this was the one. A warm feeling came over me, and I knew I had found my new friend.

When I felt alone and needed a friend, I reached for my adorable orange giraffe and gave it a squeeze. It instantly made me smile as I squished its soft body against mine. It kept me company while I ate and helped me through difficult feelings. It filled just enough space in my heart that I could continue to walk away from ED and listen to recovery. Grab on to something.

<u>Recovery Tool:</u> Tangible objects

<u>Recovery tools within the chapter:</u> Listening to Recovery

Reflections—Questions and Exercises:

As ED leaves you, finding something positive to help fill the void is a healthy step whether it be a stuffed animal, a trinket, or a book. What are some items that help fill your void? How do they make you feel when you grab on to them?

GOING OUT TO EAT

Going out to restaurants always posed a challenge for me. When I was under ED's control and ventured out to a restaurant, I became extremely anxious, obsessive, and fearful. I only went to my safe places, the places where I knew the menu. I never went anywhere new. That was against ED's rules. Now that I was in recovery, I needed to face my fear and anxiety and begin to live life like normal folks, which included venturing out to different places to eat. I needed to continue to move forward and experience the joy of trying new foods and eating in public.

To help me conquer the fear of going out to eat, I addressed it head on with recovery in mind. So I committed to going out to a restaurant (with supports) a minimum of once a week. Some weeks it was more often. I remained committed to eating according to my meal plan, no excuses. I gave input about where we would go but was not to choose any of my safe restaurants. Eating at those restaurants would be a behavior-based choice, and I needed to stay away from that. Going to those places would only be beneficial to ED, not to recovery.

To help with anxiety and fear at the restaurant, I used conversation with my supports to help me through. We caught up on each other's days and the goings-on for the weekend. It was great to laugh and gossip with them. It helped me stay in the moment instead of concentrating on the lies that ED was trying to tell me. Hearing supports helped to drown out ED's voice.

I also carried with me an affirmation stone that I placed next to my plate so I could look at it for support. My stone was multicolored, the size of a quarter, and had the word "Believe" written on it. Sometimes I picked it up and held it tightly in my hands for extra support.

Deep breathing also helped relieve my anxiety and fear while I looked at the menu. I checked in with my supports when choosing a meal to be sure I was following the voice of Recovery, not ED. I also took this opportunity to try fear foods. If we were sitting in a booth, I always positioned myself on the inside so I felt secure. I had supports all around me. If I sat on the outside of the booth, I felt too exposed. I also said a positive mantra over and over: "I am in control, I can do this, I am okay."

Going out each week helped lessen my anxiety and fear, and I slowly began to get comfortable. And before too long, I actually looked forward to going out to eat with friends and family.

Recovery Tool: Go out to eat

Recovery tools within the chapter: Deep breathing, tangible objects, positive mantras, distraction (conversation), eating with supports, socializing, following a meal plan, eating a fear food, laughter

Reflections—Questions and Exercises:

What feelings are you faced with when you go out to eat? Face the fear and regain control. Make a list of restaurants that you would like to eat at or make a list of restaurants that ED doesn't allow you to go to. Ask a support or two to commit to going with you each week. Then, make a list of tools you can utilize to help you during dinner and put them into play when the need arises. The more you go out to eat, the stronger you will get. Before too long, you will look forward to the opportunity to go out to eat—and you'll enjoy it too!

RECOVERY POSTER

Sometimes I found myself feeling down and tired during the day from the hard work I was doing in recovery. Recovery was tiring, and at times I got depressed and thought I would never recover. I wanted it to be over already. I wanted to be better now. I knew that wasn't the reality, but it's how I felt nonetheless. To help pick me up, keep me focused on my goals, and continue to keep me motivated through the times of depression, I decided to make myself a recovery poster.

Over a few weeks I gathered up magazines and cut out pictures and words that I related to. I also collected affirmations and quotes that were meaningful to me. I bought a piece of bright pink poster board, markers, glitter, stickers, and glue and set out to make my recovery poster. I wanted this poster filled with everything and anything that made me smile, gave me encouragement, and brought motivation back to my spirit.

It was a Saturday and the sun was shining as I gathered up all the pieces and sat down to make it a reality. I opened the sliding glass door and a breeze was blowing in, which gave me comfort. I set myself up at the kitchen table, turned on my music, and had my favorite beverage (Dunkin' Donuts coffee) by my side. I was ready to go.

One by one I placed the items on my recovery poster and smiled with each one. I had pictures of my dogs, pictures of my family, special quotes, affirmations, a picture of Vegas, a picture of the sun; I stuck stickers all around it, I made designs with the markers and many more embellishments. It was filled with my hopes and dreams, all of which were within reach because I was learning to live my life without ED in it.

When I was done, I looked at it and smiled with pride. It made me feel empowered and gave me a vision of what I was fighting for. I took that poster and went up to my bedroom and hung it on my closet door. My closet door is the first thing I see when I wake up and the last thing I see when I go to bed. I wanted to be sure I placed this poster where it would impact me. Having it there was the perfect place. I would start and end my day on a positive and empowering note. With strength and love inside my heart and soul, I was ready.

Recovery Tool: Recovery poster

Recovery tools within the chapter: Arts and crafts, music

Reflections—Questions and Exercises:

What do you "look" to when you are feeling discouraged, down, or in need of motivation? Can you "see" your dreams and aspirations? Gather some images that are special to you and your recovery and make a poster of your own so you can begin to "see" what can and will happen for you. Where will you put your poster so you can be sure it will inspire you?

YOGA THERAPY

When I was in treatment we had yoga classes each week. These classes showed me how to relax and how to be in tune with my mind and body. I really took to it. It helped me connect with my body and mind, even just for a moment. Because yoga had a positive and calming effect on me, I decided to add it to my recovery plan and began taking classes.

Deep breathing and quieting my mind helped me disconnect from negative thoughts and put forth a healthy vision. It helped me escape from the negativity that took up space in my head. The breathing, along with the poses, helped me connect my mind and body by bringing calmness and serenity into my life. When I felt calm, my mind was open to accept new, healthy possibilities. I was centered and my soul was refreshed.

I was able to take what I learned and use it as a tool in my recovery. I pulled out what I needed depending on the situation I was faced with. Whether I did deep breathing, a yoga posture, or meditated, I used what I needed to help me through difficult moments of anxiety, stress, doubt, or fear. Centering myself when I was having a tough time brought me back to reality where I was able to gain a healthy perspective.

Yoga therapy is a way to calm yourself down, connect with your body, and escape from the hectic daily rituals that we call life. It brings you to a quiet place where it is just you and the universe. Your mind, body, heart, and soul become one, and you can begin to see and feel the real you.

<u>Recovery Tool:</u> Yoga

<u>Recovery tools within the chapter:</u> Deep breathing

Reflections—Questions and Exercises:

Calming yourself helps relieve anxiety and fear. Yoga is a tool to help you. When you are faced with anxiety and fear and ED is talking to you, what can you do to calm yourself down and escape? What would help you? Would you listen to music, do yoga, breathe deeply? Write down five ways to help yourself get calm, find stability, and just be present.

HONESTY

Life was a bit hectic as the holidays approached, and I was stressed out at work. ED was talking to me more often and wanted me to play by his rules and not Recovery's. Because I was stressed out about work and being around all that food at holiday parties, he was finding my weakness and vulnerability and moving on in. I listened to him sometimes but defied him other times. Because of my defiance toward him, I knew I still had the will and want to fight him off.

Christmas had just passed, and Rachel and I were on our way to see an exhibit at the Museum of Science. We had one place to stop first—my session with Bob. I was eager to talk with Bob because I felt that I was getting in some trouble with ED. I was concerned and knew it was a red flag. I knew what I needed to say, but I was nervous. It didn't help that ED was telling me I didn't need to say anything and everything was fine.

At my session I came right out with all honesty and told Bob, "ED is getting in my way, and I am scared because my meal plan, my mood, and my thoughts are becoming altered. I'm afraid that ED won't let go of me and that I will follow him wherever he wants to lead me."

Bob said, "Let's figure out a plan."

Bob and I chatted about what I was doing to get in ED's way (positive self-talk, calling supports, eating with supports) and about other tools I could use (journaling, arts and crafts) to put ED in his place. After talking and crying over what I was going through, he asked me, "What do you think about going to treatment for a short while—for a bit of a boost?"

I looked right at him and said, "Can I think about it?" Surprisingly I did not say no, and I really wanted to think about it. I left that session and told him I would call him later that night with my answer.

After my session, Rachel and I continued with our plans at the museum. During our outing I thought about what may lie ahead—more treatment, leaving my family, and people realizing I was in treatment again. After seeing the exhibit, we grabbed a bite to eat and chatted about Bob's question. Guilt started to take over as I thought about doing something for myself yet again. I thought, how can I be so selfish? I was also afraid because I knew ED was right around the corner, waiting to grab me. I did not want that to happen. As I opened up about how I was feeling, Rachel said without hesitation, "You should go, Cheryl; it will only make you stronger." It was confirmation that I was not alone in my fight. That sealed the deal.

Not wanting pass up this opportunity for more help, without much hesitation or heavy thought, I made the decision that I would go to treatment for a "tune-up." I excused myself from the dinner table and told Rachel I'd be right back. I took my phone and walked outside into the cold air. People were walking in and out of the mall, milling about and doing their thing—and I was doing mine. With confidence and no fear at all, I dialed Bob's number. I said, "Bob, I'll take you up on your offer for treatment."

He said "Great, I'll make the arrangements. They will call you tomorrow." And with that, I went home and packed.

It was the week between Christmas and New Year's Day, and I had the next ten days off from work. Going into treatment was not how I wanted to spend my time off, but I knew it was what I needed to do to continue showing ED I meant business and wanted him gone forever. Going in for a tune-up would show my strength, determination, and will to get better, and it would show ED who was really in charge of my life—ME!

The next morning my cell phone rang and I wondered, was this the call I was waiting for? I answered and it was Bob. "Be here at 1:00 PM," he said.

I replied, "Will do, thanks." And so it was done. I was on my way to treatment for a tune-up.

I felt different this time when I walked in. I was not embarrassed that I was there again. I actually held my head high and acknowledged all the hard work I had done to get me to this point. I was that much further along in recovery, and I was happy to have this opportunity to get back on track and to continue to show ED who was boss. I was not going to waste a single second of it.

During this visit to inpatient treatment, I reflected on the past year and what I had learned about myself, ED, and life. I shared those thoughts during groups and with new friends. We all chatted about what was working for us and what wasn't. We exchanged ideas and bounced new ones off each other.

I rang in the New Year in treatment and used it as a motivator rather than looking down on myself for where I was. I was sure this year was going to continue to bring me to recovery and bring me experiences I would not soon forget.

Recovery Tool: Honesty

Recovery tools within the chapter: Keeping outpatient appointments, talk therapy, inpatient treatment, reflection, going out to eat, talking back to

ED, eating with supports, journaling, arts and crafts, communicating with supports

Reflections—Questions and Exercises:

Needing a "tune-up" during the recovery process does not equal failure; it equals strength. Have you found yourself in need of a tune-up? Are you being honest with yourself about your struggles with ED? What could you do to give yourself that boost to keep going? What would a tune-up look like for you?

THOUGHTS BOX

Recovery is filled with all sorts of emotions—the good, the bad, and the ugly—all of which are okay to feel. When we are struggling with ED, we are often numb to our emotions. But as we move forward in recovery, we learn it's important to feel our feelings and deal with them appropriately rather than run to ED. Feeling feelings is necessary in order to move along the recovery path.

There were many times that I was filled with negative emotions as they were all jumbled up inside me and trying to get out. Whether it was anger, frustration, or disgust, I wrote them all down on paper. Sometimes I wrote a letter to ED telling him that I hated him, other times I just wrote random words about how I was feeling or a bunch of scribbles to just get it out. The important thing was getting the negative emotions out of my system by feeling them, expressing them, and accepting them as they came up rather than running to ED. Writing them down also lessened my anxiety.

In order to completely expunge and separate myself from those negative emotions so they couldn't harm me or my progress, I came up with a way to let them go. One Saturday I went to my local craft store and purchased a wooden box along with paint, glitter, stickers, and stencils. I returned home with all my goodies, put music on, and sat down to decorate my box. When I was finished it was very festive looking, which was great because I knew it was going to hold some intense feelings.

As I got my negative feelings out and down on paper, I brought them to my box. Before I placed them in, I either ripped up the paper into small pieces or crunched it up in my hands while letting out a sigh. Doing that released more energy and emotion, and I was able to get it all out of my system. I then placed it in the box, closed the cover, said "see ya," and walked away. I knew then the negativity couldn't hurt me or hold me back anymore because I had acknowledged it, felt it, accepted it, and then expunged it from my body without turning to ED. I felt free.

Recovery Tool: Thoughts Box

Recovery tools within the chapter: Writing, arts and crafts, music

Reflections—Questions and Exercises:

Do you have a Thoughts Box or another healthy way to rid your body of the negativity that could be holding back your recovery? How do you deal with negative feelings now?

Make your own Thoughts Box. Buy a box and all the fun craft supplies and decorate it. Find a place for it to live, and visit it each time you have any negativity you want to get rid of. Feel it, accept it, and express the final emotion of it out loud as you place it in the box to say good-bye. After you walk away, check in with yourself and write down five words that express how you are feeling.

MASSAGE

Lying naked on a table while someone rubs you down is a luxury for most. For me, it's therapy. Being in tune with and connected to my body is important in my recovery. I must learn to live in this body and accept it, no matter what its size. Lying on the massage table helps me to accomplish that.

I go to my massage therapist, Erin Sweeney, every other week. She knows about my history with ED as well as how I see my body. One would think it would be excruciating for a person with an eating disorder to lie naked and have someone touch the very thing you despise; however, for me it brings me courage, freedom, strength, power, and acceptance. It took time and courage for me to get to that point, but when I was ready to take the risk and push through the fear of exposing myself and my body, the reward was well worth it.

I get naked, lie on the table under the covers, take a deep breath, and it begins. For the ninety minutes I am on that table, my mind and body become one. Sure, for the first thirty seconds ED tries to jump in and tell me that I am so big that all my fat is hanging over the table—but I talk back and tell him he is jerk and I am not fat at all. I reframe the negative thoughts into positive ones, and before I know it, my mind is in tune with what Erin is doing. I can honestly say the time I spend on that table brings me a sense of freedom—freedom from my negative body image and negative thoughts.

I lie there and actually feel my body from the inside out. I feel light all over, and I can feel the energy that is inside. I do not judge myself. I feel my body to be the instrument and gift it is. It is not my enemy, and massage therapy helps me see that, helps me feel that by being mindful and in tune in both mind and body! When I leave that tranquil space, I am ready to face the world with a sense of power because I know that my mind and body are learning to become one—to become friends.

Recovery Tool: Massage

Recovery tools within the chapter: Talking back to ED, deep breathing, reframing

Reflections—Questions and Exercises:

Learning to connect with your body is difficult, but you can accomplish it. Think about your body. Do you have a positive relationship with it? Are you connecting with it or ignoring it? Write down three ways you could connect with your body in a positive way.

USE YOUR SENSES

Some days ED is in my head and won't let go. I try to shake him off, but he hangs around to see what I will do. Will I listen to him or won't I? He tells me I need to listen to him to get through my day. He also tells me if I don't listen to him, my body will expand like a balloon and nobody will want to look at me.

During times like this, I work on my positive self-talk as well as talking back to ED, but sometimes I need a little bit of a distraction to give my mind a jolt. The jolt gives me just enough of an edge to think of something positive and healthy. To help me get a jolt, I use my senses of touch and smell.

Touching something that has a texture to it gives my mind an alternative place to go. The feeling in my hand goes through my body, and before I know it, my mind is concentrating on the texture and feel of the object. I have a couple of items I use to help me out. I have a pillow with soft fringe and a squishy, gel-filled ball with spines on it. I also carry with me a smooth marble heart and an affirmation stone. If I am feeling anxious, I might go for the soft feel of the pillow or a smooth stone. If I am feeling angry, I will grab the gel ball and squeeze the heck out of it. All of these things help distract my mind from ED's words and let Recovery chime in.

I also use my sense of smell to help me out. When I feel anxious, frustrated, or angry, scents bring my senses inward and center me. They are soothing and give me the sensation of being hugged. After I feel that comfort, I feel a sense of power and strength, like I can go accomplish anything. I keep various scented objects—candles, incense, air fresheners from my car, scented oils, and even food—close by so they are right there for me when I need them. Some of the scents that help me are lavender, clean cotton, the smell of fresh laundry, strawberry, wood, baking bread or cookies, and my favorite—coffee.

All of these things give me just enough of an edge to keep ED at bay and let Recovery chime in and take over. This way I can partake in healthy thoughts and behaviors.

Recovery Tool: Touch textures

Recovery tools within the chapter: Smell scents, talking back to ED, positive self-talk

Reflections—Questions and Exercises:

Your senses are with you at all times and can be quickly utilized to your benefit. Do you have a favorite smell or texture that can help give your mind a jolt when ED is in the way? Look around the house and grab a few things. Touch them, smell them. How do they make you feel? Choose a few that make you feel happy, safe, and secure or otherwise just completely command your attention, and keep them handy for when you need them.

SECTION THREE: BREAKING THE CHAINS— SEPARATION AND STRENGTH

ROLE-PLAYING—SEEING THE SEPARATION

As I mentioned previously, I read the book *Life Without Ed* and was very intrigued by the way Thom Rutledge worked. Through browsing his Web site (www.thomrutledge.com), I found information on the "Divorcing ED Workshop" run by Thom Rutledge, Jenni Schaefer, and Julie (Jules) Merryman. I was very interested, but the workshop was being held in Tennessee and I was in Massachusetts. Did I want to spend the money and take the risk? ED was telling me I was fine and that I didn't want or need what they were offering. He was also telling me that I did not deserve to go, I would be the fattest one there, and everyone would be staring at me and laughing.

I yelled back at ED and said, "No ED, you don't know, I know—so leave me alone!"

After much debate with ED and lots of email support from Jules, I decided to attend the workshop. I sent in the fee, booked the hotel, and jumped on a plane not knowing what was in store. It was surreal. There I was going alone to Nashville for an eating disorder workshop, all in the hopes it would help me in my recovery. A thousand questions ran through my mind. I wondered if I would find what I was looking for, if it would change my views, if it would provide me with strength. Would I meet new friends? Could I do this while ED was screaming at me every step of the way? I knew was in for a tough weekend and hoped I was prepared.

I arrived at the workshop with nineteen other women from all walks of life. We may have been different people, but we had ED in common. We could relate to each other in ways many other people couldn't. No explanation was ever needed.

Thom, Jenni, and Jules set up the room with all the comforts of home—big pillows on the floor, blankets, music, low lighting, and snacks and beverages. It was very comforting and warm right from the moment I walked in. It felt like a big hug.

Even though I referred to my eating disorder as ED, I still was not able to fully separate myself from him. I was still intertwined with him. After all, ED has been with me my entire life, and I did not fully know who Cheryl was without him. I was still a prisoner. I hoped this workshop would help me see and feel the separation between the two, even for just a second. I never expected to get what I got!

It was Saturday, and it was hot and sunny. I walked into the room with new friends and a spring in my step. My body and mind were wide open to receive whatever Thom, Jenni, and Jules wanted to give me. I was there to do the work to help me grow.

When the workshop began, Thom said, "Let's do some role-playing." I said to myself, role-playing, what the heck is that? I didn't understand at first, but then it became perfectly clear. We formed a circle around Jenni and Thom. Jenni played herself and Thom played the role of ED. I was not sure what I was about to see and was nervous but intrigued at the same time. This role-playing was new to me. I wasn't sure what to expect. Then it all began, right in front of me. The scenario and the words being spoken were all too familiar.

ED's words were so persistent, so degrading, so bossy, and so manipulative that it hit home hard for me. ED was trying to control Jenni, but she was fighting back. She said, "I don't need you ED, leave me alone."

ED tried to take her back by telling her, "You need me, Jenni. We are friends and I won't disappoint you, I'm here for you."

Jenni stood her ground and was strong and said, "NO, I'm not listening to you anymore, ED."

I sat there staring at the two of them with my eyes wide and my mouth hanging open. I couldn't believe what I was seeing and hearing. It was all becoming so clear and evident. The words, the threats, the responses, the fight was all being played out—live—right in front of me. The realization I was having was overpowering. It felt like someone came running toward me, grabbed me by the shoulders and shook me hard while looking into my eyes and screaming, "Wake up! Do you see it now?" I was there at that moment with an open mind and I finally saw, through Thom's exercise, that I am NOT my eating disorder. ED *is separate* from me. I was stunned. It took me a minute to compose myself. I was in disbelief. I thought, did I just see what I think I saw? Is this real?

Seeing the battle that I fought every minute of my existence played out right in front of me gave me a sense of power as my own person. I knew right then that I was not ED and ED was not me. I had something and someone to fight instead of fighting against myself. From that moment on, I had new hope and strength, and I decided to figure out how to use that to my advantage to fight for myself. Trust me when I tell you that you are *not* your eating disorder!

<u>Recovery Tool:</u> Role-playing

<u>Recovery tools within the chapter:</u> Talking back to ED, taking risks, an open mind and heart, recovery workshops, trust, intrapersonal therapy

Reflections—Questions and Exercises:

Knowing and believing that you are not ED is a key in your fight for freedom. See the separation. Let's work directly from Thom's exercise. Ask a member of your treatment team or a strong support to role-play with you. Have them play you and you play ED, then vice versa. Converse with each other and hear the dialogue between the two. As you practice this, it will become easier to distinguish between yourself and ED. You will see that you two are separate; you are not the same. If role-playing is difficult or can't be done, then write down on paper the conversation between you and ED. By doing that, you'll see the separation between you and ED. You are not your eating disorder.

THE FIVE MESSAGES EXERCISE

I never expected to get another "Aha" moment from the workshop, but the "Five Messages" exercise provided just that. Thom's instructions were to write down five messages ED says to us. We were to put our name in front of each remark. These are the five messages I wrote down:

1. Cheryl, you will only be successful and liked if you stay loyal to me.
2. Cheryl, you can't eat that because it will make you fatter.
3. Cheryl, I am the only one who matters in your life; everyone else doesn't.
4. Cheryl, you are fat and ugly.
5. Cheryl, you and I are connected as one because we've been together for over twenty-two years, and that commitment to each other should not be broken. You'd better not leave me because I wouldn't leave you.

After we wrote our messages, we broke into groups. We were to each listen to ED's remarks being spoken to us by another group member. We could position support people around us where we wanted, and we could also tell ED where to sit. I put ED diagonally in front of me on the left as that is where ED postioned himself and spoke from my entire life. It was my turn and Jenni, who was overseeing our group, asked if she could show me something that worked for her. I said, "Sure, I'm open to it." She moved closer and sat back to back with me. While ED's remarks were being read to me, I had my supports around me and my support behind me holding me up, which was very empowering. I was strong and did not retreat back in fear. I couldn't because I was being supported from behind. I was right in ED's path, yet I was able to stand up and be strong. I was not alone.

Later in the day we had a continuation of the exercise in which we were to write down five recovery messages (even if we did not believe them at the time). Here are mine:

1. Cheryl, being in recovery shows strength.
2. Cheryl, you are well liked and loved.
3. Cheryl, trust your treatment team.

4. Cheryl, it does get better.
5. Cheryl, a friendship with food is a positive thing.

We then broke up into groups and spoke these "recovery" messages out loud. At the end of our recovery message, the group said "Cheryl, this is true." Again, we chose where our Recovery voice as well as our supports would sit. When it was my turn I said to Jules, who was overseeing our group, that I needed Jenni to be a support for me. I said that because she was behind me when ED spoke to me, I needed her behind me when Recovery spoke. It needed to come full circle for me.

Jenni joined the group, and I placed my supports around me. I had my Recovery voice on my diagonal right because that is the direction from which I always hear it, and I put the others in my group all around me. Jenni then positioned herself back-to-back with me. I reached back with my hands and grabbed hers. The exercise began.

I heard the voice of Recovery coming at me with gentle force. When we got to the part where the group said "Cheryl, this is true," it really hit home for me. I heard the words of Recovery coming at me—but more important, I felt the strength behind me holding me up to be strong to fight. I could feel the vibrations of Jenni's voice as she spoke the words, "Cheryl, this is true." Her hands clenched mine as the words were spoken. I could feel her strength, hope, and truth move through my body and touch deep inside my heart and soul. My body felt like it had been struck by lighting. It felt numb yet alive all in the same moment. I was literally "feeling recovery." I was experiencing it through the energy of another, someone who's been through it. I was being given the power and hope I needed. It was a gift.

The exercise was over and we all dispersed from our groups. The day was coming to a close, and I was overcome with an overwhelming sense of hope and strength that I had never felt before. I had heard and felt Recovery, and I knew it could be done.

Before I knew what was happening, my entire body began to shake, my insides were heavy, my eyes began to fill up, and my heart was overcome with emotion. I was vulnerable. In a matter of a moment, it all came out as I broke down and sobbed right there in front of everyone. I couldn't control my emotions. I felt like my body was filled with light that was pulsing throughout my entire system. Everyone came to my aid and held me tight. All I could say was "I can do this, I really can do this. Thank you."

I left that weekend with a desire to fight through to victory. I left with new friends. I left with hope. I left with strength. Being a part of Thom's workshop and meeting everyone there had been more than I was looking for and more than I ever expected. It was my turning point.

Recovery Tool: Five Messages exercise

Recovery tools within the chapter: Honesty, an open mind and heart, acceptance, crying, recovery workshop

Reflections—Questions and Exercises:

Try Thom's exercise. Find a quiet place and write down five statements that ED says to you and then five statements Recovery says to you (even if you don't believe them yet). Gather a few supports or take them to your support group or therapist and have them read back to you. Listen closely, take it all in, and experience it. Feel the power and hope of recovery around you. Feel your strength. Know that you can recover. It is possible.

RECOVERY REMINDERS

While at the workshop I found out about the Life Without ED jewelry collection. The collection was created by Sue Gillerlain (in partnership with Jenni), jewelry designer and founder of www.sarah-kate.com. I was lucky enough to be able to purchase a necklace while at the workshop. The flower on this necklace became a symbol of strength for me. It hangs close to my heart and gives me strength when I need it.

Because of the power and depth this flower possesses for me, I wanted to make it a permanent fixture in my life. I wanted to be able to look at it when I needed and have it as a tool to help me. So, I decided to have the flower tattooed on my body. The symbol of strength and recovery and my experiences at the workshop would always be there for me to see, remember, and feel. I needed to put it in just the right spot.

Without hesitation, I knew exactly where to put it. I would have it tattooed on the inside of my left ankle. In the past I had practiced self-injurious behaviors on that portion of my body. I wanted to place my flower there so it would always remind me to be strong and take care of myself rather than hurt myself.

I got the name of a tattoo artist from a friend and called him up. He informed me that he was going to be at a tattoo convention the following week and it would be fine if I wanted to come see him then. I told him what I wanted, and he said it wouldn't be a problem at all.

Saturday came and I woke with excitement in my belly. I was pacing all around the house and was very jittery. I couldn't contain my excitement. The convention didn't start until late afternoon, and the day seemed liked it took forever to go by.

Finally the time came to leave. The convention was over an hour's drive, so we packed up and headed out. As we reached the parking garage of the convention center, my stomach started to do flips. My excitement was hard to control. I was fidgeting with joy and anticipation. I was so excited that my hands were tingling.

Rachel and I walked into the hall and made our way to the artist's table. I told him who I was, and he said, "Glad you're here, have a seat. What do you have for me?"

I took my necklace from around my neck and told him, "I want this flower on the inside of my left ankle."

He took the charm and did his magic. Within five minutes he had traced the flower on my ankle and asked, "How's this?"

"Perfect," I said. "Let's do it." And away he went.

As he was doing his thing, pride filled my body and I was smiling from ear to ear. I was proud of myself for having the strength to get where I was and doing all that I had done. I was winning the fight. Within half an hour it was on my body forever, and I could not have been happier. I walked away feeling powerful and protected. All I have to do is look down, and there it is, staring right up at me. I had a permanent weapon against ED!

<u>Recovery Tool:</u> Recovery reminders

<u>Recovery tools within the chapter:</u> Wearing motivational jewelry

Reflections—Questions and Exercises:

Weapons against ED come in many forms from jewelry to posters to tattoos and others. Look in your arsenal; what are some of your weapons against ED? What significance do they have for you in your recovery? If you don't have any, go get some!

TALKING TO ED

As I mentioned in the chapter "My Treatment Team," I contacted Thom Rutledge after his workshop to see if he could take me on as a client and join my treatment team, which he gladly did. My first therapy phone session with Thom took place on a ninety-degree day in July. My belly was doing flips as I dialed the number. I wondered, how is this going to go? Will it be weird? Will I get something out of it? The phone began to ring, and then I heard, "Hello, this is Thom."

My voice quivered a bit as I said, "Hi, Thom. It's Cheryl Kerrigan."

The conversation began and so did the session. We chatted about the work I had done at the workshop. We chatted about my recovery steps thus far, and then he asked me something that threw me for a loop.

He said, "Would you be willing to role-play? I want to talk to ED."

I replied, "I've never done that before. I don't know if I will do it right."

He reassured me and said, "If you are open to it, it will just happen. ED will be there."

With fear in my voice I said, "Let's do it." And so it began.

My heart was beating out of my chest as he asked the first question.

"ED, what are your intentions with Cheryl?" he asked.

"To make her happy, of course," ED replied.

"How do you make her happy, and what is your relationship with Cheryl?" Thom asked.

"I've been with Cheryl for a long time, Thom. I know what she needs and wants, you don't!"

"ED, how do you know what's best for her?"

"I just do."

"That's not an answer. I want specifics," Thom continued.

"You are so stupid, Thom. You don't know what you are talking about. She needs me."

"No she doesn't, ED. You are wrong."

Thom was persistent and gave it right back to ED. Thom did not back down. Right from the start ED was on the defensive and gave Thom attitude. When Thom asked ED for specifics or to explain himself, ED lashed out with insults and lame answers. ED did not like to be questioned. He tried to show Thom that he was in charge, but Thom would not give him that role. The role-playing went on for about fifteen minutes.

After role-playing, Thom gave me his feedback, which blew my mind. He told me that when ED speaks, his voice is low and monotone. He also said that ED carries himself like an overconfident asshole. I was shocked to hear how Thom described ED. I did not realize that ED actually sounded different than me and had that persona. How would I? ED had never spoken out loud to anyone else before. He had only spoken to me.

Thom asked me to listen to ED's answer to the next question and concentrate on the sound of his voice.

"ED, what have you done for Cheryl today?" Thom asked.

"I do everything for Cheryl, Thom. Leave us alone. You don't know anything."

After ED answered, my eyes were wide with shock as my mouth hung open and I screamed, "Oh my God, Thom, I can hear him, I can really hear him!" I could hear how ED's voice *was* different than mine and how he *was* acting like an overconfident asshole. I could feel it and hear it for the first time ever. I was totally freaking out. I was amazed!

My first session with Thom went great. I had gone out on a limb and role-played for the first time and truly learned from it. I had an open mind and an open heart. I hung up the phone with a smile on my face and couldn't wait until we would talk again.

Recovery Tool: Talking to ED (role-play)

Recovery tools within the chapter: An open mind and heart, intrapersonal therapy

Reflections—Questions and Exercises:

While you're living with ED, you never really get the chance to hear him live and in person. You listen to what he says, but you don't actually hear him. The next time ED wants to talk to you, let him talk out loud and record him. Have him say what he wants and then be sure to come back with a positive statement after he speaks. Listen closely. What does your ED sound like? Write down what his voice is like and what his tone is like. Knowing what he sounds like will give you the knowledge to differentiate between you and him. You'll have more power.

MUSIC

Hearing words of encouragement and stories of my reality at just the right moment is the connection music gives me. It helps me through difficult times and gives me the strength to forge ahead. If I am having a hard time or need an extra boost of confidence, I turn the radio or my iPod on, and bingo, I have a song there for me in an instant. During the day, I use my computer to listen to music online so I'm never in silence. If I can't get to a radio, I hum or sing a favorite song.

Music is a motivator for me. I use it to give me the extra push I need to get me through. It relaxes me too. I pick and choose certain songs to help me depending on the situation. As my recovery progresses, new songs are added to my playlist. Music brings me into the zone of my reality, my work of recovery. Turn on the radio and see what songs speak to you. Here are some songs that help me along my way:

"When You Put Your Heart In It" by Kenny Rogers
"Keep Holding On" by Avril Lavigne
"Life Without ED" by Jenni Schaefer
"Bye, Bye" by Jo Dee Messina
"Keep the Faith" by Jo Dee Messina
"Believe" by Josh Groban
"This Will Be (Everlasting Love)" by Natalie Cole
"Proud" by Heather Small
"Stronger Woman" by Jewel
"Beautiful" by Christina Aguilera
"Free" by Elliott Yamin
"All I Want To Do" by Sugarland

Recovery Tool: Music

Recovery tools within the chapter: N/A

Reflections—Questions and Exercises:

When you are faced with difficult moments and having a hard time, what music do you gravitate toward to pick you back up and get you back to thinking positively? Is it rock 'n' roll, rap, country, or Top 40? What speaks to you? Take a listen and see what your mood does when the first note is played. Make a list of five songs that you can add to your recovery toolbox. Start a "recovery boost" playlist on your iPod or computer and listen to the songs daily to give you the extra encouragement to keep moving forward.

AFFIRMATIONS

During recovery there are many moments when an extra lift of encouragement or positive thoughts are needed. Reaching out to supports is great, but they may be unavailable sometimes. In order to keep myself on track and in the right frame of mind, I decided to carry with me words of encouragement so I could pull them out anytime I needed.

I went to some of my favorite Web sites to get affirmations I could write down on paper. I printed them out in fun colors, then I got out my index cards, stickers, markers, and tape and went to town. I decorated the cards and taped my affirmations to them. Not only was it good to see the affirmations while I was doing the project, but the project itself was also healing and relaxing. Concentrating on the project at hand got my mind off the daily grind. Arts and crafts do that for me, so it was an added bonus.

To be sure I had my affirmations around when I need them, I kept some in my purse, my briefcase, and at home. Anyplace I was, I could pull them out and get affirmed!

I wanted to see something positive everywhere I went. My vehicle takes me everywhere I go, so that was the perfect thing to outfit with an affirmation—a vanity plate. So I thought carefully about the message I wanted to portray to my psyche and to the world, and I came up with BY BY ED. I ordered my vanity plate through the motor vehicle registry, and it arrived in a few weeks. Each time I get in and out of my vehicle, I look at that message, and it is confirmation of my continued commitment to recovery. I read it with pride in my heart and dedication in my soul.

Not only did I carry affirmations around with me, I also said them out loud to myself every day. I wanted to hear my voice speak kind, positive words back to me. Before I started doing it, it was suggested to me to stand in front of a mirror and say the affirmation while looking at myself. Because I struggled with a bad body image, looking at myself in the mirror posed a challenge. I did not want this positive action to turn into a negative one, so I thought long and hard about how I could do this without the risk of triggering myself at the same time. Then it came to me.

I decided it was important for me to look into my eyes while speaking because they are the window to my soul, so all I needed to see in the mirror was my eyes. I had a solution: I pulled out my hand mirror and took a peek. Lo and behold, I could see my eyes. From that day on, I pulled out that mirror, looked myself in the eyes, and spoke one positive word after the other while looking into the window of my soul. Here are some of the affirmations I use:

1. I have faith in my process of recovery.
2. I am strong. I have the power. I can decide.
3. One step at a time. That is how I will get where I'm going.
4. I deserve to recover. I am worth it. I can do it.
5. BEAT ED.
6. Food is my friend, not my foe.
7. Do what it takes.
8. I am in the right place at the right time doing the right thing.
9. Believe.
10. The process is worth the reward.
11. Live for the moment.
12. Life is good.
13. Live life, don't just merely exist.

Recovery Tool: Affirmations

Recovery tools within the chapter: Arts and crafts, positive self-talk, index cards with affirmations, speaking daily affirmations (in mirror)

Reflections—Questions and Exercises:

Surrounding yourself with positive thoughts helps when the negative thoughts arise. What are some of your favorite affirmations? Where can you put them so they are accessible to you when you need them? Your car, your bedroom, your office, your journal—what places fit into your daily schedule? Begin each day by looking at yourself and speaking a positive affirmation. A positive thought is powerful in your fight for freedom.

TRUST

ED was in my face more than usual lately and was annoying me with all his talk. It seemed difficult at times to step out of his way. I found myself listening to him here and there and my behaviors did not go unnoticed. Rachel and my treatment team were tuned in to what was happening and were there to help and offer advice.

At a session with Bob, he was talking to me about ways to continue to step in and regain full control. He was concerned that ED would gain my attention and take me back. I sat in the chair across from him and listened to what he had to say. He said, "One sure way to regain control would be evening treatment, Cheryl."

"I don't need any more treatment, I am totally fine," I said. "How much treatment does a person have to do? I know what I am doing." He explained to me his concerns, and I told him I wasn't interested, but I would think about it if he wanted.

"I'll check in with you tomorrow," he said.

The next day I went about my day and headed home after work. Rachel was working late that night. It was just me and the dogs, so I had the quiet I needed to think. Rachel and my treatment team were telling me that evening treatment would be a good addition to my recovery, but I wasn't so sure. After all, I was only listening to ED here and there, which wasn't so bad, right? Wrong!

I was sitting on the sofa watching TV when the phone rang. It was Bob. I knew he was calling to check in on me and to see if I had decided to include evening treatment in my recovery plan.

"Have you thought about what I said?" asked Bob.

"Yes, and I have decided that I don't need to go to evening treatment," I replied.

"Did you decide that or did ED?" Bob asked.

"I did. I'm totally fine, you are blowing things way out of proportion. I've had enough treatment already, I don't need it!" I exclaimed.

"Cheryl, you are listening to ED and you need to continue to find things that interrupt that. Evening treatment will help you find ways to continue to interrupt the behaviors," Bob replied.

"You are being unreasonable and unfair; you don't know what you are talking about, I am fine," I screamed.

We bantered back and forth for a good five minutes and then Bob said something that shook my core. He said, "Cheryl, if you are going to continue to listen to ED and not your treatment team, then you and I will have to take a break from working together. I am not going to be a part of ED's team."

His words hit me like a baseball bat to the stomach. I sat in the chair in shock. My eyes filled with tears, and my voice quivered as I asked him, "Are you serious?"

"Yes, I am," he replied.

The thought of not having Bob scared me. He had been there with me from the first day of my recovery. I thought, what is going on? What am I doing? Is this really happening?

ED chimed right in and told me, "Cheryl, you don't need Bob anyway, you only need me. Get rid of Thom too, and then we can be together. Everything will be fine."

Then Recovery chimed in and said, "Cheryl, listen to Bob. He knows how to help you. He is telling you the truth. I promise. ED is giving you bad advice."

ED and Recovery went back and forth and I cried to Bob the entire time. Thoughts were swirling around in my head, and my emotions were out of control. Fortunately, Recovery was becoming louder than ED, and I was hearing it loud and clear. I knew I had to take the leap and take the control back before ED could. And so I did. I said to Bob "Okay, I trust you. I'll do it. I'll do evening treatment."

We wrapped up our conversation and I hung up the phone. I sat on the floor, patted the dogs and thought, it can't hurt. I can only gain more knowledge in my fight against ED, right?

Recovery Tool: Trust

Recovery tools within the chapter: Talk therapy

Reflections—Questions and Exercises:

As you go along in your process of recovery, do you find yourself listening to ED here and there? Has ED regained your attention? Is he taking you off the path? Be honest with yourself and write down three ways that ED may still get you to cooperate with him. Has a support brought it to your attention? Trust your support, not ED. What steps will you take next to help keep ED away and you on the correct path? Don't let ED take you back—stay strong!

EVENING TREATMENT

It was Monday afternoon and my workday had ended. Fall was in full swing, and it was dark and cold outside. I was tired from my day but instead of going home for the night, I was headed to evening treatment. I work in the same town as the treatment center, so the drive was short. I pulled into the parking garage and made my way to the familiar building ahead.

As I walked toward the building ED was saying to me, "Cheryl, why are you doing this? We don't see each other that often. What's the problem?" I said to him, "ED, I don't want to see you anymore, but you keep coming around once in a while and that's a problem. Just leave me alone." I walked into the building with my head held high, ready for whatever would come.

Evening treatment was in the same space as day treatment, so I was familiar with the surroundings and the staff. I opened the door to find five other patients anxiously waiting for the evening to begin. I went in with an open mind and willing to gain more tools to fight ED. As I sat down in my chair, I smiled at the others and said hello. We exchanged hellos and soon we were chatting up a storm about our days, our struggles, and the week ahead. It was comfortable right from the start.

Evening treatment took place from 5:30 PM to 8:30 PM three nights a week—Monday, Tuesday, and Thursday. First we had group therapy based on either of two therapy models: dialectical behavior therapy (DBT) or cognitive-behavioral therapy (CBT). Group therapy was followed by a supervised dinner and then a process group.

We got weighed once a week (we didn't see the number) and had our vital signs taken. In addition, we met with a social worker to go over any issues or problems we were having. A nutritionist was also available to us if we needed support or had questions regarding our meal plan. We had worksheets to fill out daily regarding the meals we ate offsite as well as our feelings and struggles.

We were required to bring our dinner with us to evening treatment. This helped us by giving us an opportunity to plan a "meal on the go" that kept us to our meal plans. It was good practice. We were checked before we started, and we all ate together in the group room. Conversation or music was always present during dinner. It was a relaxed environment as we all sat and enjoyed our time together. After dinner we usually did some distraction before the next group to help us with the discomfort of having eaten dinner.

We played games, meditated, listened to music, or just chatted about plans for the week.

Then we had a process group. At this group we were able to pose questions to other patients or to the staff, brainstorm with others on ways to interrupt ED, or talk about problems or issues we were having. We could basically use this time for anything we needed. I found that even if I wasn't in the mood to talk, by the end of the group I realized that I had gotten involved and chatted the whole time. It was very interactive and a helpful tool.

Evening treatment gave me the extra support I needed to continue to see the path of recovery and get ED out of my way. It was nice to have this structured environment to go to and be connected to others like me. We were all in different stages of recovery but all wanted the same thing—to get rid of ED. I very much enjoyed the DBT group and found it very helpful at this particular time in recovery. It brought me inside myself and forced me to be silent within. It helped me to push negative thoughts aside so my mind could be quiet and still.

When evening treatment ended, I was armed with more strength to fight ED and win. I had more ammunition to use against him, and I was ready to continue the fight. I was feeling confident and had a spring in my step as I felt excited to put what I learned into action.

ED was pretty aggravated and ticked off and tried to get my attention, but I was getting even stronger and my words and actions of recovery were getting louder. ED realized that I was not going to give up on recovery. I am a fighter, and I am going to win!

<u>Recovery Tool:</u> Evening treatment

<u>Recovery tools within the chapter:</u> Talking back to ED, DBT, CBT, meal planning, support groups, music, socializing, following a meal plan, playing games, eating with supports

Reflections—Questions and Exercises:

Getting extra help in your fight against ED can be a very powerful addition. Think about your recovery process. Is ED standing in front of you at times, preventing you from moving forward? What extra help or support would fit into your recovery plan?

RENAME A FEAR

I will never forget it—I remember exactly where it happened, and I was scared to death. It was a Saturday around 11:00 AM and I was at Erin's on the massage table. It all happened in an instant; I was relaxed one minute, then the next minute fear and anxiety rushed through my body as I experienced something that had not happened in a long while. It was hunger.

At first ED jumped right in and told me to ignore it, told me I was stronger than hunger and that all I had to do was listen to him and he would make it go away. He told me all I had to do was to listen to his instructions to be back on track again and to feel normal. I gave ED the floor to say what he had to say, and then I put a stop to it.

ED was lying, and I told him so. I told him to shut up and that I was not going to listen to him on this. I reframed his so-called logic and put it into verbiage that was real and made sense to me for recovery. I told him that hunger was a feeling that "normal" people experience and it did not mean I was bad or had done anything wrong. On the contrary, it meant I was doing something right: I was getting healthy.

I knew that if a hunger pain had come once, it would come again—and I needed to be prepared for it. I needed to have something ready to quickly make it about recovery before ED could creep in and try to take over. After I thought about it, I decided to rename my hunger pains. Now I call them "recovery nudges." Calling them recovery nudges is a positive, healthy twist on something that is scary for me to feel.

When a nudge comes along, I know my body is functioning properly and getting itself back to working order. It is telling me what I need to do for it to heal. It needs to experience recovery nudges in order to keep me strong, healthy, and on the path of recovery.

Recovery Tool: Rename a fear with a recovery twist

Recovery tools within the chapter: Talking back to ED

Reflections—Questions and Exercises:

What fears are you faced with in your process of recovery? Write them down and then rename them so they have a positive spin. When a fear is replaced with a positive thought, it is easier to get through it. It's not so scary. What do you come up with?

SUPPORT GROUPS

Being committed to recovery means doing *whatever* I need to in order to recover. With that being said, I knew it was time for me to go "see" Thom, not just talk him over the phone. We set up three consecutive appointments, each an hour and a half long. I was headed to Nashville and wanted to make the most of it. I called it my "Trip Toward Recovery."

From the minute I decided to go to Nashville, ED chimed in and was telling me all sorts of lies, trying to convince me that I shouldn't go. He said, "Cheryl, you are so stupid; you do not know what you are doing. If you care about me, you won't go." He even told me I would get lost down there by myself, so I should stay home. He tried to maneuver his way in, but I was determined to be stronger than he was.

I said, "ED, shut up and stay out of my way. I know what I'm doing and I don't need your help. So leave."

Knowing Nashville had lots of recovery help to offer, I let my fingers do the walking and started planning my schedule. I knew this trip would be intense and tiring but knew it would be worth it. *I* was worth it!

I found out that Jenni Schaefer was going to be speaking at a Finding Balance (www.findingbalance.com) support meeting in the Nashville area on one of the nights I was going to be there. I called, got directions, and told them I would be there. I was excited to see Jenni again and to meet new people. Plus, I wanted to show Jenni my tattoo!

Next on my agenda was to find an Eating Disorders Anonymous (EDA) meeting (www.eatingdisordersanonymous.org), and within seconds of visiting their Web site, I was happy to see they had a meeting happening in Nashville while I was there. My recovery support groups were all planned out. I had an open mind and was excited for the trip.

To maintain balance, I also made sure I planned some fun and relaxation. I booked a Discover Nashville Tour and a massage during my stay. Staying balanced is key. I had a little bit of this and a little bit of that to do while in Nashville. I had a well-rounded trip planned, and I was ready.

<u>Recovery Tool:</u> Support groups

<u>Recovery tools within the chapter:</u> Talking back to ED, self-care, commitment

Reflections—Questions and Exercises:

Support groups can be a good way to share feelings, brainstorm, and receive hope with others that understand your struggle. What has been your experience with support groups? If you haven't attended one, why not? Is ED standing in your way? Do a little research and find a support group to attend.

TAKE RISKS

It was Monday morning and I awoke filled with hope and excitement as I thought, today is the day I leave for Nashville. By this time tomorrow, I'll be in Thom's office working my butt off. I got out of bed and went about my normal morning routine of coffee, breakfast, the morning news, and a shower.

I had made a plan the night before that I would start my trip off with a bang: I would have my morning snack at the airport, a bagel and cream cheese (fear foods of mine). As you can imagine, ED was talking to me the entire morning. He told me if I ate that, then I wouldn't fit in the seat of the plane. I wondered, how stupid does he think I am? I know that's not true, but he is hoping I will have a weak moment and listen to him as I've done in the past. I told him, "Not today, ED. I'm choosing recovery, not you."

I got to the airport and checked in. I made sure I had plenty of extra time to eat—and enjoy!—my bagel. I proceeded through security and walked toward my gate. After a few short steps, I saw it—my favorite place, Dunkin' Donuts!

My heart was racing as I got my money from my purse. I thought, I can't believe I'm doing this—I'm going to get a bagel! I stood in line waiting patiently for my turn. As I stood there, ED called me fat, called me a loser, and told me I was being stupid. I told him I knew what I was doing and I didn't want to hear what he had to say. I told him he was wrong.

Before I knew it, the lady behind the counter said, "Can I help you?"

I smiled and said, "Yes, you can."

With my bagel and coffee in hand, I walked over to my gate, took a seat, and thought, I am ready for this; I can do it! To help relieve my anxiety, I pulled out my iPod and prepared my bagel. There it was, staring back at me, asking me to eat it—and so I did. I took one bite after another. I was relaxed and entertained as I listened to my music and looked around at all the people milling about. After I was done, I texted Bob and told him about my success. I wanted to share my good news. And by the way, it was delicious. I highly recommend it.

The flight attendant announced over the loudspeaker that we were ready to board. I boarded the plane bound for Nashville—another step toward recovery (boy, recovery is expensive!). I wish I could say I boarded that plane alone, but ED came along for the ride. He was very angry that I was going to Nashville and doing things to support my recovery. He was talking in my ear the entire trip, trying to convince me I did not know what I was doing and that I would fail doing it. I told him to shut up and continued on my quest, one foot in front of the other.

I checked in to the hotel and unpacked my suitcase. I had the day ahead of me free to explore. I love country music, so I was excited to be in Music City, USA. However, I had to take care of first things first—and that meant lunch. I was a bit nervous because I didn't know what places to eat were around, but I pushed the nervousness aside by doing some positive self-talk.

I walked out of the hotel, walked around the corner, and right there in front of me was a sandwich and soup place. Perfect! I walked up to that counter with nerves of steel and placed my order. I was determined, not nervous. I grabbed a table by the window so I could see the sites and do some people watching. Vanderbilt University was right next door, so college students were all around. It brought back memories. I was tempted to compare my body to theirs but quickly pulled out my journal to help me with the anxiety I was feeling.

Evening came, and it was time to head to a recovery meeting. With my directions in hand, I climbed into the cab and off I went. The next stop was the Finding Balance meeting. We made our way through the streets and highways of Tennessee. Twenty minutes and sixty-five dollars later, I arrived (did I mention that recovery is expensive?).

I was welcomed with open arms into a warm and comfortable place. The meeting was held at their offices, which were in an inviting ranch home. It was filled with cozy furniture, burning candles, the smell of coffee in the air, and warm friendly faces throughout. It put me at ease right away. I didn't even feel like I was far from home, it felt safe.It was great to see Jenni again. Before the meeting began, we chatted and laughed. I showed her my new tattoo, and she was impressed. The meeting began and Jenni told her story. Question and answer time came, and a relaxed atmosphere made for a great night.

After the meeting we all grabbed some beverages and chatted about our process, our hopes, and our dreams. It was nice to be connected to others who were in the same fight I was.

I headed back to the hotel with hope and strength running through my veins. I had a great night. I laid my head on the pillow and smiled as I closed my eyes and clutched Moo Moo. I couldn't wait for the next day to begin.

Morning arrived, and I was going to have my first face-to-face session with Thom. I was so excited—excited to see him again and excited to get to work.

As I opened the drapes, there was a knock on my door. It was room service. I opened the door, and in came a man with my breakfast. As I sat and ate breakfast, the sun came through the window and shone on my back, comforting me while I ate. It felt like warm arms wrapped around me. Even though I was alone, I felt supported.

After breakfast, I jumped in the shower and got ready for my day. I left the hotel and walked to Thom's office, one step at a time further along in recovery. I reached my destination and opened the door into his tranquil space.

As I walked in, I immediately felt comfort and hope in my heart. I was in the right place. I felt excitement in my belly and couldn't wait to begin. I took a seat on the sofa in his waiting area. On the end tables on either side of the sofa were books he had published and various reading material. The wall in front of me was filled with articles, cartoons, posters, and affirmations. To my left was a small kitchen with a sink, a table, and a microwave.

Within minutes I heard a door to my left open, and out he came. "Hey Cheryl, how ya doing? Welcome," he said.

Smiling from ear to ear, I got up from the sofa and said, "Hi Thom, I'm doing great."

"Let's get started," he said. I followed him through the door into his office and took a seat. I was ready and raring to go. We were happy to see each other, and we were both ready to do some work.

As I sat on the sofa in his office, I looked around to get a feel for the place. After all, I was going to be spending the next few days here. In addition to the sofa I was sitting in, there was a chair to my left and a chair to my right. There was a small table next to the chair on my right, so I figured that was where Thom would sit—and I was right. The wall in front of me held a bookcase filled with books, figurines, and other various items that I figured he used somehow in his work. There were pictures, posters, affirmations, and other pieces of art all over the walls. His office was warm and cozy.

The door shut behind him and the work began. The session was intense, but I learned a lot about myself and ED in just one day. Here are some points and messages I took away from that meeting:

- The essence of my relationship with ED is "brainwash."
- My relationship with ED is all one-sided; it's just his way or no way.
- ED doesn't care about me, he only wants me to do what he says.
- I have to take full responsibility to change this. Don't blame ED, take responsibility.
- Recovery is strong, firm, tough love. Feel that energy.
- I am not close to perfect; no one is perfect.

I left with homework to do and a day of work ahead of me. I pondered what I had learned about myself during the session, what I had learned about ED during the session, and what I had learned about my recovery during the session. I was open to the newfound knowledge and the hard work ahead.

When I left Thom's office I came across an old-fashioned diner and soda shop. It was lunch time, and I thought about going in and eating lunch that included fear food. ED quickly interjected and told me how bad it would be if I went in there and ate anything risky. He told me I did not need to eat lunch because I had eaten breakfast and told me to keep walking. I told ED to shut up, that I am in recovery, that I hate his guts, and that I need to take risks to get rid of him. I told him he was a liar and then walked into the diner for lunch.

Lunch was a major accomplishment that should not be forgotten. I didn't listen to ED at all, and I ordered two risk foods—a BLT and an ice cream milkshake. Aside from the guilt and shame I felt about eating these, it also felt liberating and it was actually yummy. I did some journaling to help with my thoughts and also talked to the staff. I sat at the counter so I would be able to engage with others. I didn't isolate. I had disobeyed ED and gotten what I wanted to eat. It felt great! I walked back to the hotel with my head held high.

The next two days were filled with my sessions with Thom, doing homework, eating risk foods, and having a little fun in between. I wanted to be sure I balanced myself, so I booked a massage one of the days and a tour of Nashville the other day. It was great to meet other people and get to know Nashville and its history. It was exciting to go to the Country Music Hall of Fame. I had a good time.

I want to share with you some more messages and points that came from the other sessions with Thom. I taped my sessions and listened to them again during the day, and I wrote down the work I did. I wanted to have it in writing so I could look back on what had taken place. Here is some of what I learned:

- Celebrate milestones (like eating risk foods, etc.).
- You are supposed to eat more than your meal plan. The meal plan is only a minimum requirement.
- Take ZERO advice from ED.
- Be prepared. Have a plan. You never want to be without appropriate caution.
- Don't be a victim.
- Commit to recovery. Do it over and over. There are no breaks in recovery.
- Your life is about you, not ED.
- As you separate from ED, you gather your own identity.

- You are not ED.
- "Can't" versus "won't": It's not that you can't do it, it's that you won't do it.
- Don't debate with ED.

My last night in Nashville was upon me, and I was going to an Eating Disorders Anonymous meeting. I gathered my things and left the hotel. I got my bearings and began walking north. The ten-minute walk from the hotel was quick and filled with thoughts of recovery. I arrived at a white house on the corner and walked around the back to enter.

After a few flights of stairs, I reached my destination. There were chairs placed around the room as well as pillows to sit on. There were lamps on end tables and meeting material for us to take. It was a small, intimate group of women, all of whom had one thing in common—ED. The meeting began. It was great to connect with others who share the same fight. Even in another city, I was still surrounded by support.

The next day, I opened my eyes from a restful sleep and realized it was time to go back home. I had done a lot of work and wanted to keep it going, so I ordered a risk food for breakfast and enjoyed it as I watched the *Today Show* in my room.

As I boarded the plane home, I knew I had made a lot of headway. I had taken many risks and pushed myself during this trip. I felt good about moving forward and getting stronger. ED was very mad, and I was very excited. I know when he is mad that it's confirmation I am working my recovery. I had learned a lot about myself and found out that I am stronger than ED. I had reaffirmed that recovery is possible, and I am doing it. I have what it takes!

Recovery Tool: Taking risks

Recovery tools within the chapter: Intrapersonal therapy, talk therapy, talking back to ED, music, going out to eat, journaling, support groups, disobeying ED, self-care, following a meal plan, positive self-talk, eating fear food, fun activities

Reflections—Questions and Exercises:

Taking risks shows ED that you are not afraid and you are in control, not him. It's one way to move forward and leave him behind. Write down five risks that you want to take and then write down three steps that can get you there. What risks have you already taken?

PROTECT YOUR INNER CHILD

At one of my sessions with Thom while I was in Nashville, we talked about protecting my inner child. We chatted about how the little girl inside still looked up to ED and still viewed him with wide eyes. We spoke about how ED is a destructive babysitter and how in the past, adult Cheryl had let the little girl down and had not protected her from ED.

According to Thom, the inner child represents the parts of ourselves that have been disappointed, hurt, or even traumatized by early life experiences. By creating a strong, loving parental voice to speak to the inner child, we begin the process of healing those wounds. Thom said that creating a healthy inner parent to care for an inner child is the best metaphor for becoming an independent, self-caring adult.

On that day, Thom said we needed to try to enlist the trust of my inner little girl and show her that ED is not a good companion for her. She doesn't know any better and needs to be shown other avenues. We needed to show her love and guidance. We needed to protect her from ED's lies. I had let her down in the past but needed to show her that I love her and want her to be safe and happy.

For homework, Thom asked me to write a letter from adult Cheryl to my inner little girl. Before I sat down to write the letter, I had some thoughts about what I wanted to say. I didn't want to scold or try to convince her ED is bad for fear she would retreat from me and I would lose her forever. I just wanted to tell her the truth, and I hoped and believed the truth would come through. I hoped that in the end she would trust me and be able to see that I truly love her and want to help her. I wanted to show her that I am strong enough to protect her. I was scared she wouldn't listen and wouldn't give me a chance because I had let her down and abandoned her before. I wondered, will she trust me? After sorting out these thoughts and fears, I sat down and wrote my letter.

Dear Little Girl:

I am sorry I was not there for you when you needed me the most. The pain and suffering you have gone through and are going through is not your fault. I am here for you now, and I will take you under my wing and protect you for a lifetime. I will fix it. Come with me; you will find strength, happiness, safety, contentment, love, and hope. I will help you fight the lies ED tells you and will show you the truth. The truth is inside you and just has to be set free. I will show you freedom. You can count on me to be beside you forever. I won't let you down. I love you.

Cheryl

Writing this letter to my inner little girl helped me experience compassion for myself. After all, I would never want to hurt either one of us. It was powerful. It was something she needed to hear and something I needed to say and face so I could move forward.

Recovery Tool: Reach out to/protect your inner child

Recovery tools within the chapter: Honesty, writing, talk therapy

Reflections—Questions and Exercises:

Think about your relationship with your inner child. What is the relationship like? What would you say to her? Sit in a quiet place and reflect on the relationship between you two. Grab some paper and a pen and write down the words you would say to her.

FACE ED HEAD ON AT MEALS

When I first began my recovery, I wanted to be as far away from ED as I could during mealtimes. I wanted to keep him away from me so I could try to eat in peace and get through each bite. He was overwhelming to be around, and I just wanted him away from the table. But as time went on, that changed.

During one of my sessions with Thom, he pointed out to me that I needed to face my fear during mealtimes and show ED who was boss. He said to take a stand and look him square in the eye so he knew I meant business. I needed to gain more courage to fight him off and continue to move forward.

To help me do that, Thom suggested an exercise. He told me to actually set a place for ED at the table and have him sit with me while I ate. This way I could look right at him and tell him with confidence and force who was in charge. I told Thom it would be hard and scary for me to do, but I would give it a shot.

So at my next meal, I set a place for ED. I gave him a placemat, napkin, plate, knife, fork, and a glass. I set his place straight across from me so I could look at him head on. I was a bit nervous because I wasn't sure what he would say or how I might react, but I was prepared. I fixed my plate and sat down to dinner. There he was, right across from me with a big smile on his face. He was so smug and so cocky! He thought things were going to be like they used to be. Boy, was he wrong!

Before he could start talking, giving me his usual spiel about how fat I was getting and how I was doing something wrong, I said with exaggerated drama, "ED this food is sooooo good. It's cooked perfectly and I love it!"

He rolled his eyes at me and said, "You're fooling yourself; you know it's horrible and you shouldn't be eating it."

"You have no clue what you're talking about, and frankly, I couldn't care less what you think," I snapped.

As I sat there and ate dinner, I responded to each of ED's negative comments with a positive comment and, more important, a bite of food. As I continued to eat, ED grew quiet. The message was becoming clear: Watch out ED, here I come! He was beginning to realize that he couldn't stop me— and perhaps more important, so was I. He still tried, but I dominated the conversation and the situation. Now *I* was the force to be reckoned with.

As the weeks went by, I continued to set a place for ED at every meal. But I started to notice his presence was deteriorating. My strength was overpowering his. He had no reason or desire to sit with me anymore. He had lost his grip. I was in control.

Recovery Tool: Face ED head on at meals (and dominate)

Recovery tools within the chapter: Talking back to ED, following a meal plan, talk therapy

Reflections—Questions and Exercises:

Set a place for ED at your own table. What feelings came up for you as you set a place for ED at your table? When you sit down, what will you say to him? What kinds of things does he usually say to you? Write down three positive comebacks that you will use to defend yourself if he tries to keep you from enjoying your meal.

JOURNALING

When you're faced with difficult times and you choose healthy behaviors instead of unhealthy ones to cope, it is a sign of recovery and progress.

Our fourteen-year-old dog Maxie had cancer. She had a total of four surgeries to remove tumors from her mouth. She had her ups and downs and was still puppy-like at times. She was a smart, loyal friend. She made me smile. The unfortunate time came when we had to make the very hard decision to let Maxie go. The day was sad, difficult, and draining. We had lost part of our family, and the grief was overwhelming. A part of me was gone.

I wanted to rid my body, soul, and mind of all the sadness I was feeling over Maxie's passing, and my thoughts went to ED. I wanted to run to him so badly so he could take away my pain and make me numb again. I knew that if I went to him, the feelings of sadness would disappear. But at what cost?

Running to negative behaviors makes *all* the feelings go away—good ones *and* bad ones. Negative behaviors make you numb. I had to remember that eating disorder behaviors are bad and feelings are good—no matter what the feeling. I needed to feel the sadness and work through the pain with recovery in mind. Only then I would know I was still going forward.

I did end up feeling all the feelings that Maxie's death brought. I did not run to ED. He wanted me to come to him, but I stood my ground. I told him NO. I had to trust the process and trust recovery. Even though I didn't want to, I continued to eat my meals and snacks and felt the pain with each bite. It was overwhelming, but I did it—one second at a time. I cried a lot both for Maxie and myself and used friends and family to help me through.

I used my journal to get my painful thoughts out. I wrote down my memories of Maxie, and I wrote about the pain I was feeling now that she was gone. My tears fell on the pages with each word I wrote. I also wrote Maxie a letter in my journal to let her know what she meant to me. My journal was a place to release all my emotions, both happy and sad. When I wrote my feelings down and got them out, a sense of calmness and relief ensued. I could express myself in a healthy way rather than running to ED.

I was proud of myself that I actually felt it rather than being numb to it. More important, I was working through it. Using negative behaviors brings numbness, and being in recovery brings feelings to the forefront. Feeling is what I strive for, and feeling feelings equals progress.

Recovery Tool: Journaling

Recovery tools within the chapter: Talking back to ED, following a meal plan, crying, talking with supports, trust

Reflections—Questions and Exercises:

Learning to cope with feelings is part of life and part of recovery. What feelings have you experienced lately? Did you want to run to ED as they came up? What healthy behaviors did you or could you use to cope with the feelings? List three things that you can use to help you deal with feelings in a healthy way.

WEIGHT GAIN

It was a Friday night around 8:30 PM when the phone rang. I could see on the caller ID that it was Bob. I thought, What could he want? I answered the phone with a question: "Hi Bob, is everything okay?"

"I want to check in with you on a few things," he said. He talked to me about my upcoming nutrition appointment with Amy and then about my latest appointment with Dr. G, my medical doctor. He said, "I have some good news, Cheryl; you reached your goal weight." His words came at me like a burst of cold air right to my face. They took my breath away and my heart skipped a beat. First came fear, then came pride—fear because I knew ED would be very mad and I needed to be ready for him, and pride because I had worked so hard to get there.

After I got off the phone with Bob, I sat for a few moments in my dark home office and thought about the message he had given me. It was a message that angered ED but brought me a sense of joy. Knowing that was confirmation that I was beating ED. When ED is mad it usually means Recovery is stronger. I was proud of myself. I had worked hard to gain that weight, and it paid off.

Hearing those words—"you reached your goal weight"—was bittersweet. I was happy because I had worked hard to reach my weight goal, but ED immediately began screaming at me, "Cheryl, you are a fat loser and you disappointed me." I knew that was not true, and I told him so.

I said, "ED, you don't know me anymore, and I don't even like you, so go away."

He got angry with me and told me I was a failure. He said, "Cheryl, all you have to do to get back to normal is do what I say." It was tempting and at some points I wanted to believe him, but I knew deep down he was lying. ED could only give me loneliness, despair, depression, sickness, feeling worthless, and so on, and so on, and so on. What he was dishing out was not what I wanted. Not anymore.

I said to him, "ED, I'm not listening to you, you don't know what's best anymore. Go away. I am proud that I reached my goal, and nothing you could say will change that."

Hearing those words, "you reached your goal weight," gave me a sense of power and freedom—power because I am beating ED and freedom because I am learning to live my life without him in it. I am doing it. Bring it on!

Recovery Tool: Weight gain

Recovery tools within the chapter: Talking back to ED

Reflections—Questions and Exercises:

What thoughts and feelings were you faced with when you heard the words "you reached your goal weight"? Were you anxious, scared, proud, or driven? What action did you take after hearing the news?

A WORKOUT BUDDY

Overexercising had been a problem for me in the past, and when I began my recovery, I was told to stop until I was healthy enough to continue. It was very difficult, but I listened to Dr. G and stopped going to the gym. Now that my body is at a healthy weight, Dr. G has given me the go-ahead to exercise. It had been a long while since I had exercised, and in the past exercise had been a negative behavior that took its toll on me. Even so, I know that exercise in moderation is essential to optimal health. I knew I would need help and a plan to control my urges to overexercise, so I made one. I wanted to be proactive, not reactive.

So, on the days I decided to go to the gym, I asked a support to go with me. I needed a workout buddy there to guide me and show me what is normal and when enough is enough. Having a workout buddy with me helped to reel me in and teach me how much exercise is appropriate and to keep me focused. It was nice to be able to chat with someone as I worked out and check in with someone on my routines and movements.

If I didn't want to go to the gym sometimes because it was triggering, I put in a workout video and worked out to that. I had help obtaining those videos. To help protect my recovery, I ask a support to go to the store to buy me a few videos. I gave them guidelines about what I was interested in and let them go from there. This protected me because I wasn't able to obsess about the all videos available and have it be a triggering event. I had various tapes to choose from, so I wouldn't get bored watching the same one over and over. Workout videos were good for me because when the video was done, I knew it was time to stop.

Because the gym could be a trigger for me, to protect myself and my recovery I also hired a personal trainer to come to my house to teach me the proper way to work out and get healthy. I had a trained professional to guide me and keep me motivated and on track. She knew about my background, so my program was built for strength training, not weight loss (as were all my workouts).

Another tool I used to help me control the urge to overexercise was taking an exercise class. I take yoga. When the class is done, so is my exercise for the day. Taking a class also helped to me socialize and make new friends. It was great.

I had a plan in place to protect me from the urge to overexercise yet help me stay healthy, and it worked. Balance is key—in both recovery and life.

<u>Recovery Tool:</u> A workout buddy

<u>Recovery tools within the chapter:</u> Timed workouts, personal trainer, socializing

Reflections—Questions and Exercises:

To help keep yourself and your recovery safe from overexercising, what types of timed exercise could you do? Would you try kickboxing, yoga, or an aerobics class? Remember, only exercise when you get the okay from your doctor.

POSITIVE SELF-TALK

It was a Saturday afternoon, and I jumped into my Jeep and headed to the mall. I had a Tiffany's gift card that was burning a hole in my pocket. After my Tiffany purchase (two silver rings), I walked around the mall. After a bit, I found myself standing in front of one of my favorite clothing stores, Ann Taylor. I stared at all the beautiful clothes inside, wondering if I should go in.

Clothes shopping usually brought me nothing but panic and despair. I thought, am I strong enough? Can I do this? Will I even have the courage to try anything on? Will I feel I deserve it? As I stood there like a lost child looking for her parent, a wave of strength came over me and I said to myself, "I can do this. I deserve some new clothes." After all, I knew I reached my goal weight, so I was safe on that account. It was about time I got an outfit or two.

Usually, trying on clothes for me is anxiety provoking and a trigger for eating disorder thoughts. Also, my bad body image gets in the way of me actually buying anything. Guilt also plays a part. I feel guilty buying myself things, so when it comes to the moment of purchase, the negative thoughts usually win. But this time, I was determined to win the argument—on all fronts.

I walked around the store with wide eyes, grabbing various sizes of one thing after another and tossing clothes over my arm. While I shopped I said to myself, "I am worth this and I deserve nice things." I had plenty to start with as I headed to the dressing room to try it all on. As I shut the door behind me, my heart was pounding and my breathing was rapid; I was filled with anxiety and uncertainty. I thought, will I feel comfortable? Can I do this? Will they look good on me? Oh God, help me! I got through the moment by taking a few deep breaths and saying over and over, "I'll be fine, size doesn't matter, I love my new body." I put one foot in and then the other as I pulled pants up my bare legs, past my hips to my waist. I stood alone in the secluded dressing room and realized that if I wanted to make this experience even more real, I would need to walk outside and look at myself head on. I had come this far and nothing was going to stop me. So I said out loud, "Let's do this," and I took the plunge. I walked outside of my confined, safe dressing room and stood in front of the three-sided mirror.

As I looked at myself, negative thoughts arose for a quick second—but so did good thoughts. I felt pretty good in what I was wearing, and I thought I looked nice. I liked the way the outfit fit my new body and was happy with the look I had chosen. I said to myself, "Damn, I look good."

As I was looking at myself, a sales assistant came to see if I needed anything. We began talking about the clothes I had picked out and she said, "I'll be right back, I want to get you something." A few minutes later she came back with more clothes in hand. I was a bit overwhelmed but also glad to have help figuring out what actually looked good on me. It's always better for me to have help with shopping; that way, I am almost forced to purchase something for myself. She handed the stuff over and I began the task of trying it all on.

I came out of the dressing room wearing a beautiful gold cashmere sweater and gray dress pants. I liked the looked but thought the pants were too tight. I was used to hiding my body and not wearing anything that actually fit. The concept of clothes actually fitting me was all new. The sales person came over to me and said, "You look great. That outfit fits you perfectly." I expressed to her my thoughts on the pants and she told me that they looked like they were made for me. I went back into the dressing room and did the sitting down and bending test and logically they did seem to be okay. I wondered, can I get past the fact they fit me rather than hide me? Will I feel too exposed?

I tried on the other outfits, and I felt good about myself. I looked at my body at various angles and did not judge it as much as I used to. Don't get me wrong, ED was there and was talking and yelling negative things to me, but I talked back and told him to shut up.

After I was done trying on all the clothes, guilt began to take over and thoughts started to emerge, like "I don't deserve any of this" and "how can you be so selfish." I needed to take control of the situation and have a reality check, so I sat in the dressing room and practiced positive self-talk. I told myself, "You worked hard to gain this weight and get healthy. You deserve to reward yourself with something new!"

I am learning to live in the moment and at that moment, I felt good about myself. I felt good in those clothes, and I used that to my advantage. I took that feeling and ran with it. I gathered my stuff, walked up to the register, and had the cashier ring me up. I did it, and I deserved it—and I bought those pants too!

Recovery Tool: Positive self-talk

Recovery tools within the chapter: Deep breathing, positive mantra, talking back to ED

Reflections—Questions and Exercises:

As you make your way through recovery what activities, events, or trips that ED has kept you from are you looking forward to doing? Perhaps clothes shopping? Reward yourself and use positive self-talk to help you through. Make a list of places, and as you experience them, journal about how you felt before, during, and after. Then cross it off your list and move on to the next one.

BODY MANTRA

As my body was changing and becoming healthy, I wanted to find something to aid me in the ever-so-difficult feat of accepting my new vehicle. I wanted something positive to say each time I saw myself in a negative light or if I was having a bad body image day. So I decided to come up with a body mantra. I figured that saying (or should I say singing) this mantra over and over would help to convert the negative thoughts to positive ones. So I sat down armed with paper and pen and got to work.

The exercise was a success. Not only did I come up with a body mantra, the exercise helped keep my thoughts focused. I was less obsessive and my thoughts didn't go to any unhealthy places. I was focused on what I was doing and enjoying the challenge. In the end, my mission was complete. I had a mantra, and I was ready to put it to use. Here is what I came up with:

> I love my body, oh yes, I do
> I love my body, and it is true
> B-O-D-Y, body, body you rock the sky
> "B"eautiful
> "O"utstanding
> "D"edicated
> "Y"ou
> Go body, go body, go body

Is my body mantra silly? Sure, it's quirky and it won't win any awards, but it does its job and helps me through difficult times. I sing this mantra when bad body image thoughts race through my mind and I need a bit of reality. It states a truth, a truth I need to keep hearing: My body is beautiful, and so am I. Positive thoughts in and negative thoughts out.

__Recovery Tool:__ Body mantra

__Recovery tools within the chapter:__ Writing

Reflections—Questions and Exercises:

Saying positive mantras helps get the positive thoughts flowing and pushes the negative thoughts aside. Sit down and write out a mantra that will help you get through difficult thoughts or situations. Your mantra can be anything positive that speaks to you. Start writing and see what pops into your head.

TRANSFORM ED'S RULES

From the very beginning, ED had specific rules I was to follow. He told me if I followed all his rules, I would be happy, successful, loved, thin, and many other things he enticed me with. No matter what situation I was faced with, he always had a rule for me. Even if I was faced with the same scenario later on, I needed to listen closely as the rule might have changed since the last time. Listening to ED and his rules was exhausting. It took all my time and concentration to be sure I was getting everything right, but at what cost?

During one of my sessions with Thom, we spoke about ED and all his rules. Thom suggested transforming ED's rules into my own recovery rules. He gave me an example and I told him I would try. He told me not to get discouraged even if it took some time and to stick with it because it was an important factor in my recovery.

So I sat down one afternoon and wrote out some of ED's rules. I stared at them and said to myself, "These are the rules. How can they be something else?" I remembered what Thom said to me and his example of a conversion and put my nose to the grindstone. I took each rule one by one and transformed it from a negative to a positive. It took some time and practice, but after I got going, Recovery took over and it got easier.

Here are some of ED's rules and how I reframed and transformed them into my own.

ED's rule: You must eat less than everyone else.
My rule: I eat until I am full and satisfied.

ED's rule: When you go out to a restaurant, only order safe foods.
My rule: When I go out to a restaurant, order what I want and crave.

ED's rule: If you weigh enough to give blood, then you are a fat and unlovable.
My rule: If I weigh enough to give blood, then I am healthy enough to help people.

ED's rule: If you eat bad foods, you must restrict.
My rule: There is no such thing as bad foods.

ED's rule: Your skinny clothes must always be too big for you.

My rule: My clothes will fit my new body, and I will look and feel beautiful.

ED's rule: If you are in recovery, you are not special or unique anymore. You are weak.

My rule: f I am in recovery, I am strong and free.

ED's rule: If you have your period, it means you are too fat.

My rule: Having my period means my body is working properly and I am healthy.

When I wrote down ED's rules and then transformed them, I could "see" recovery start to play out right in front of me. Transforming his rules made my recovery stronger. When I saw them and read them back, I knew I had the ability to make them a reality. I could feel ED's power diminish as I became stronger with every transformation I wrote.

Recovery Tool: Transform ED's rules

Recovery tools within the chapter: Persistence, talk therapy, practice

Reflections—Questions and Exercises:

Sit in a quiet place armed with your journal or a piece of paper. Think about the rules that ED has for you and write them down. Look at them one by one and transform each rule into a recovery rule or statement. It may take time to begin to hear Recovery kick in. Don't give up. Be persistent. When you are done, read your new rules back to yourself and feel the power behind them.

THROW AWAY YOUR SKINNY CLOTHES

Every day I used to walk into my closet, grab something off the rack, and get dressed. As I got dressed, I looked around aimlessly at all the clothes I had. My eyes would always wander and linger on the top shelf. That shelf held my skinny clothes. I used to reminisce about wearing them and about what life was like back then.

One day as I was getting dressed, my eyes landed on "those clothes." As I stared at them, I realized those clothes and the feelings around them were still taking up space in my mind and heart. It was like I was holding out hope that someday I would fit into them again. I knew that would never and could never be the case, but still having them around allowed the spark inside me to be lit every time I looked at them. It gave me a sense of comfort and hope but in the wrong direction.

In order to continue to move ahead in my recovery, I knew I had to part with those clothes. I had to get rid of the bad karma they held for me. Wearing those clothes again would be proof that ED was in control and that death was near, and I certainly did not want that to happen.

The next weekend I armed myself with a large trash bag and headed to the closet. To help me with the difficult task of giving them up, I armed myself with items of comfort. I went to Dunkin' Donuts and got a coffee; I put the radio on my favorite country station and brought Moo Moo and my orange giraffe into the closet to give me moral support. I was prepared.

ED decided to chime in and said, "Cheryl, this is a mistake. You can get back into those clothes; it's possible and it can be done, just listen to me and it can happen…I know you can do it, I have faith in you." I listened to what ED was telling me and then snapped back, "ED, shut up. I am going down a different path and don't need your advice or help anymore. I'm fine on my own. I don't need you, but thanks anyway." I was firm in my statement, so he knew where I stood.

Before placing each piece of clothing into the bag, I held it up and remembered the feelings I had around it and the rules that went with it. I was a bit sad at first because I knew I would never be that size again, but then Recovery jumped in and I quickly realized that *I don't want to be that size again*. Everything that came with those clothes was all ED, and none of it was good. It was misery and despair as I was trying to live up to something that was unattainable. I want something different. I want to be healthy and happy, and recovery can give me that—is giving me that. So I said good-bye to each piece as I placed it in the bag, but I was hopeful and excited for all that is ahead. Pieces of the old Cheryl were gone as the real Cheryl took a stand for freedom.

Recovery Tool: Throw away your skinny clothes

Recovery tools within the chapter: Tangible objects, music, talking back to ED

Reflections—Questions and Exercises:

Have you gotten rid of your skinny clothes yet? What's holding you back? How would you go about getting rid of them? Would you donate them, cut them up, or throw them out with the garbage?

DISOBEY ED

Rachel and I booked a cruise to the Caribbean, and I was ready to sail away. I was excited to get away, and I was ready to relax. As we boarded the plane, I realized that ED had come with me, but he was not sitting next to me; he was in the last row of the plane. He was talking, but the sound of the engine was drowning him out, so he was easy to ignore.

We landed in Florida and had a few days before we were to board the cruise ship. We headed to the in-laws' for a visit. It was a great couple of days of having them show us around and going to all the cool restaurants. We had a fun and relaxing time. The vacation was off to a great start.

On the day of departure, we arrived at the marina and boarded the boat. We found our cabin and unpacked. I was ready for some fun in the sun. Unfortunately, my body had another agenda. The boat left the dock and the rocking began. The seas were rough and the boat rocked and swayed twenty-four/seven. Seasickness took a hold of me and would not let me go. I was surprised that I felt ill because I was wearing a seasickness patch.

ED was watching and was in tune to what my body was telling me. I was nauseous and had a splitting headache. Curling up in a ball on the bed was becoming a daily occurrence. I did not feel well at all. ED wanted to take advantage of the situation and starting talking to me. He said, "Cheryl, if you listen to me, the feeling of sickness will go away and you will be able to have a good time." I said to myself, does he think I'm going to fall for that?

I knew ED was lying and knew that if I wanted to recover, I couldn't listen to his crap. I knew for sure that I had to eat according to my meal plan and force some nourishment into me to help me feel better. I knew that listening to ED would only send me spiraling downward into a relapse. I had to be stronger than him and follow recovery.

ED was annoying and was getting on my nerves. I wanted to be on this vacation without him, and I was so angry that he came along for the ride. I knew he only wanted to see if I would have a moment of weakness where he could slip his way in and take over. I had to be stronger than him and be on alert and ready for what he was dishing out. I knew what I had to do.

Listening to ED was not an option. Continuing to eat according to my meal plan and stay on the path of recovery was the only way. Despite the fact I wasn't feeling well, I had to stick to my meal plan. It was the only way to beat ED. I told ED to stop lying to me and told him I would prove him wrong. He laughed at me but I didn't care. Days went by and I ate my meals and snacks. Not only did I push through and stick to my meal plan, I also ate fear foods.

I pushed though the seasickness and fought back. ED was not going to win this fight—I was. I was not going to let him take away all the hard work I had been doing. I want to recover, and I knew listening to him would not get me there. I had to do what I had been taught by my treatment team and trust it.

I got off that boat at the end of the cruise and felt empowered. I had won. Even though ED was there, I did not let him win. I let him talk, acknowledged him, and then completely disobeyed him. I didn't allow him to take over. I told him I knew what I was doing and I did not need his help. *I* knew what would make me feel better, not him. As I became stronger in my recovery, ED became weaker. I was working it and I was winning. I stayed true to myself and to recovery and even managed to have a good time on the cruise. Despite the seasickness, in my opinion, the vacation was a true success! *And* I wore a bathing suit! Success times two!

<u>Recovery Tool:</u> Disobeying ED

<u>Recovery tools within the chapter:</u> Talking back to ED, following a meal plan, fun activities, distraction, family, eating with supports, going out to eat

Reflections—Questions and Exercises:

Is ED whispering in your ear right now? Write down what he is telling you, and then push back and write down your recovery response. Actively disobey him. If he is telling you not to eat something, eat it. Do the opposite of what ED is telling you. By doing so, you begin to take your power back and diminish his.

RECOVERY WEB SITES

Even though I surround myself with supports and items that help with my recovery, I still find at times that I want a little bit more, that something extra. When I get that feeling, I turn to the Internet. I go to some of my favorite recovery Web sites and read about other people's stories, participate in a chat, or read some blogs. Browsing these sites gives me the extra comfort of knowing I am not alone in my journey. It also confirms everything I am going through and that everything is worth it. Recovery is worth it. Here are a few Web sites that I frequent. Enjoy!

Gürze Books (publisher specializing in eating disorders):
www.bulimia.com
Eating Disorder Blogs (run by Gürze Books):
www.eatingdisordersblogs.com
My ED Help: www.myedhelp.com
Finding Balance: www.findingbalance.com
Thom Rutledge (psychotherapist and author): www.thomrutledge.com
Andrea Roe (survivor and author of *You Are Not Alone*):
www.youarenotalonebook.com
Shannon Cutts (survivor, author, and founder of Key-to-Life and
Mentor Connect): www.key-to-life.com
Jenni Schaefer (survivor and author of *Goodbye Ed, Hello Me* and *Life
Without Ed*): www.jennischaefer.com
Something Fishy: www.somethingfishy.org
National Eating Disorders Association:
www.nationaleatingdisorders.org
My Self Help: www.myselfhelp.com
Voice America: www.voiceamerica.com

<u>Recovery Tool:</u> Recovery Web sites

<u>Recovery tools within the chapter:</u> N/A

Reflections—Questions and Exercises:

When you want and need that something extra for support, where do you go to find it? Realizing you are not alone in your thinking or fight is comforting. Do you have any favorite recovery Web sites that you frequent? If not, browse some and find support.

PUT DISTANCE BETWEEN YOU AND ED

In all the years ED was dominant in my life, I envisioned him right next to me (on my left side). Sometimes he sat on my lap and even got on my back. He knew exactly where to position himself to be effective.

As my recovery progressed, ED's position changed. In the very beginning of my recovery, he was still walking right beside me. He was pretty ticked off I was in recovery so he did not want to leave my side. He tried to take advantage of me, but I was learning not to let him. When recovery was able to come through, ED started to walk a step or two behind me—progress.

More time passed and recovery was present. At this point, I used a psychological construct to put ED in his place. I envisioned a structure in my mind—my "house"—made up of several rooms on one floor. This is where ED lived. Using this psychological construct made it easier for me to continue to separate the two of us. The rooms did not have doors but were all separate from each other. When I told ED to leave me alone, he realized I was getting stronger. He would turn around, walk away, and go into a room. I could see and feel him walk away from me, and that felt good. Sure, he came back to see if I would follow him—but our relationship was changing. I was learning how to take my control back, and I told him to get away—progress.

As more time went on, I kept adding to my "house" until it had two floors and all the rooms had doors on them. Now when I tell ED to leave, I tell him to "get upstairs." This way, even though ED and I still occupied the same space we were separated by doors, walls, and floors—progress.

When ED talks to me now, sometimes he comes into the same room as I am in; sometimes he is in a different room, so his voice is softer. A lot of the time he is in his room upstairs with the door shut, so his voice is very muffled or practically nonexistent. No matter what he has to say or where he says it, it's my response to him that matters. I respond with recovery in mind to protect myself.

Being able to see the separation is a key in recovery. I am fighting someone, not myself. ED may be in the same house as I am, but there is always a separation between us—and it's my response him that matters. If he comes to me, I have the strength and the tools to protect myself and tell him to go away—and he listens. Progress.

Recovery Tool: Put distance between you and ED

Recovery tools within the chapter: Talking back to ED

Reflections—Questions and Exercises:

Where does your ED reside? Where is he right now? Create distance between you and ED. Put him in another room or put him on an island. Think about where he would go. Has his position changed as you have moved forward in your recovery?

END THE CONVERSATION

It was a Wednesday, and I was in a bad funk and not feeling particularly optimistic. I was wavering back and forth about whether I wanted recovery or not. Thoughts like I am never going to get through this and I'm never going to recover went through my mind. I was feeling hopeless and helpless. This could have gone from bad to worse if it was up to ED.

As I battled with uncertainty and depression, ED told me all sorts of things. He said, "Cheryl, I know exactly what you need to do to feel better, you need to restrict. Cheryl, your treatment team doesn't know you like I know you. You don't need recovery. All you need is me. Come on." I was in a vulnerable state, but what ED was telling me wasn't sitting well with me. So I said a positive mantra to drown out ED's words.

As the day progressed, my bad body image took hold, and ED jumped in right away. He said, "Cheryl, you are so fat. Your treatment team is a disgrace, and they betrayed you and let you get fat. I won't let you down like they did."

As I sat there in my kitchen, I knew I had a decision to make: Would I listen to what ED was telling me, or would I listen to recovery and continue to go forward? I thought, I can turn this around! I decided to let ED finish what he had to say, and then I yelled, "ED, get to you room and leave me alone." I had to take control. I knew I needed listen to recovery and put a plan in action to help me. As Thom says, "Never be without appropriate caution."

The first part of my plan was to connect with my body, and I went to a yoga class to do that. It was nice to get into a quiet place and respect my body for the temple it is. Yoga also helped me direct my fear, insecurities, and anxiety outward. I was there just being one with my mind. I was not obsessing about anything. I was able to let everything go and relax.

Dinner was next. To show ED I was in control, I decided to make a fear food. I was alone, so I turned on the TV for distraction and fed my dogs at the same time. We all had dinner together—and I enjoyed every bite. While I cleaned the dinner dishes, I put the radio on and sang out loud to keep ED away. The dogs were howling as my voice got louder and louder. Thank goodness no one could hear me!

My mood was picking up and my negative thoughts were turning into positive ones. ED was still in his room and was trying to come out to bother me, but he couldn't get near me because I was following recovery. I was winning this fight.

To finish the night off with a bang, I decided to log on to Voice America's Web site (www.voiceamerica.com) and listen to Doris Smeltzer's show, *Savor Yourself...Beyond Skin Deep*. Hearing her message of recovery and life was comforting, soothing, and empowering (archives of the show can be found at www.andreasvoice.org).

As the day came to an end, I felt good about the decisions I had made and the plan I put in place to keep me on the recovery path. I was proud of myself and had even more confidence in my ability to fight and recover. I had used various tools and made them work for me. I was proud that I did not let ED have the last word. In the past, I had talked back to ED but I had let him have the last word. Now, I take my power back by interrupting him each time he tries to talk, putting an end to his babble. I talk over him and walk toward recovery before he can speak again. As Thom has always told me, never let ED get the last word. It is important that *you* have the last word.

<u>Recovery Tool:</u> End the conversation

<u>Recovery tools within the chapter:</u> Talking back to ED, positive mantra, yoga, following a meal plan, distraction (TV), music, recovery Web sites, pets, eat a fear food

Reflections—Questions and Exercises:

Ending the conversation with ED shows strength as it proves to him you are taking your power back. When faced with a confrontation with ED, what could you say to him to take your power back and end the conversation? Write down five messages to ED and keep them close at hand so you can pull them out when needed. Never let ED have the last word!

MEALS TO GO

It was softball season, and I was headed to the ball field after work to see my niece Stephanie play. This particular game was being held at a field that has no concession stand. It's simply a field with no frills.

This circumstance posed a question that I needed to answer: What was I going to do for dinner? Sure, ED tried to jump in and tell me I could skip dinner and not to worry about it because it was only one meal.

"Not a big deal," he said.

I knew better. Listening to ED and skipping a meal was not an option. Skipping a meal is an invitation for ED to take advantage of me and manipulate the situation to get me back. I was not going to let that happen. Plus, as Thom says, there are no breaks in recovery.

I told ED thanks for the suggestion, but I would pass on it. I told him I have a better solution: I am bringing dinner with me. I had leftovers in the fridge from the night before—filet mignon. Yummy! I went through the fridge, gathered my meal, and packed it in a Tupperware container. I tossed silverware and napkins into the bag, and I was ready.

After work I headed up to the field with my dinner in hand. ED was trying to tell me that I would look stupid bringing dinner to the field. He told me it was fine if I wanted to bring it, but in the end I shouldn't eat it.

"Everyone will be staring at you and making fun of you," he said.

I told him to shut up! I got my chair, grabbed my dinner, and headed up the hill to the field.

Familiar faces were gathered around and hellos were exchanged. Everyone was having fun. My niece was enjoying herself and was having a great game. When dinnertime came, I reached into my bag and pulled out my dinner. As I opened my container and started to prepare my food, the people around me looked to see what I was doing.

"My dinner," I said.

Everyone looked with wide eyes and turned up noses to get a whiff of what I had. The people around me began to comment on how great my dinner looked and how smart I was for bringing it. They commented on how hungry they were. They said my meal was "better than any concession-stand hot dog." I agreed and ate my dinner while I watched the game.

My plan had worked perfectly. I was able to stay on track and get what I needed. No one made fun of me as ED said they would—in fact, they were jealous. Bringing a meal or a snack with you in order to get what you need is a healthy behavior and a smart move toward recovery.

Recovery Tool: Meals to go

Recovery tools within the chapter: Talking back to ED, disobeying ED, following a meal plan, family, friends, distraction (softball game)

Reflections—Questions and Exercises:

Going places is no excuse for not fitting food in. You must nourish yourself to stay strong and be free. If you were going somewhere and needed to bring a meal with you, what would your meal to go consist of? Write down a few ideas for meals to go (according to your meal plan) and have them at the ready in case you need to use them.

A LETTER TO ED

During one of my sessions in Nashville with Thom, we role-played. I played ED and Thom played me. By role-playing this way, I was able to view myself as an outsider looking in. I was able to see and hear what was going on and make a judgment about it. Words were exchanged and questions were asked. When it was all over, I sat back on the couch. Thom asked what I thought.

I told him that ED sounded desperate and full of contradictions—desperate because he wanted me back and I was not listening. He was contradicting himself and talking crap. As I was talking to Thom, something happened that I didn't expect. I started to feel pure anger toward ED. My body language was pulling away from ED (he was on my left) and my anger was getting deeper. My hands turned to fists and a fire was inside my belly.

This was unusual for me because I had previously felt anger toward myself for listening to ED. My inner bully made me feel badly about myself and told me I was not strong because I had listened to ED. This, in turn, made me angry with myself.

On that day, I was actually feeling deep anger toward ED. I said to Thom, "How dare ED treat me that way. Who does he think he is?" I could feel the anger down to my soul, and it was finally directed at the correct person—ED.

Working off of that anger toward ED, Thom asked me to write an angry letter to ED for homework. Thom told me to put the anger out there to him and let ED hear it. That afternoon, I sat in a park across from my hotel. There were birds chirping nearby and the sun was on my back as I sat on the grass. I was ready to let it all out. I had an open mind and open heart as I felt every bit of anger inside. This is what I wrote.

Dear ED:

You are not going to like what I have to say, but you need to shut up and listen. I am angry, very angry with you, and it is real. I stood beside you my entire life, showed my commitment to you, and you pulled the wool over my eyes all the while. You lied to me and manipulated me, and you caused me misery. It is only now that I am away from you that I can see who you truly are. You don't care about me at all. You only care about yourself, the power and the control. You sicken me, and I want to be far away from you. To even look at you makes me feel sick inside. All those years you told me you cared about me and wanted me to be happy. That was a lie. All you ever cared about was yourself. I don't ever want to be with you again. You sit there and call me a lowlife and a loser if I don't listen to you. Look in the mirror ED—you are the lowlife and loser. You wouldn't know happiness, success, or freedom if it slapped you across the face. I am angry at how you treated me, the lies you told, and the control you took. How dare you! I am pissed off and I hate you. All you have done is take, take, take. You have given me nothing good—ever. You are full of shit and are nothing to me. I hope you live in the same hell you have put me through.

Good-bye,

Cheryl

I felt even more freedom after writing this letter. It was liberating to get the anger out and finally direct it toward the appropriate place. I knew right then I did not have to be angry with myself.

Recovery Tool: Letter to ED

Recovery tools within the chapter: Role-playing, intrapersonal therapy, nature

Reflections—Questions and Exercises:

Directing anger away from ourselves and onto ED is healing and appropriate. Tell ED how you feel about him and what he has done. Write a letter to ED and put it all out there for him to hear. Don't hold back. Experience all the feelings.

MINDFUL AT MEALTIMES

Night after night I sit with Rachel, eating my dinner and doing what I need to do to be healthy and to find freedom from ED. All was fine until at one point I began feeling extremely full during dinner. I was feeling bloated, expansive, and full. I was finding that I had to literally force myself to finish dinner. It was uncomfortable and I was confused. I wondered, why now, after all this time, am I feeling like this at dinner time? What is going on? Why is this happening? Is ED trying to sneak in and take over?

Sure, in the beginning of recovery it was extremely hard and painful to get through a meal, which sometimes took hours, but now that I have learned to use positive self-talk, supports, and distraction and to have faith in the process, mealtimes are much more palatable. As I sat there one night drinking my water and eating my meal, a large burp escaped me. My stomach immediately felt a release and had more room for food. I continued to eat and drink, and shortly thereafter the uncomfortable feeling overcame me again. Rather than panic or revert to an old ED behavior for comfort, I pushed onward while being mindful and paying attention to my body to help solve the mystery.

As I brought my sparkling water to my mouth, my eyes focused on the bottle—and then it came to me like a slap in the back of the head! I thought, it's the carbonation! Could that be it? I immediately switched to regular water and finished my meal.

The next night I poured myself regular water with dinner. There I sat, eating my meal, drinking my water, and feeling no ill effects. The feelings of bloating, expansion, and fullness were not present. I had figured it out! I continued the test for the next few nights and it was confirmed. No more bubbles during dinner!

Recovery Tool: Mindfulness

Recovery tools within the chapter: Positive self-talk, distractions, eating with supports, following a meal plan

Reflections—Questions and Exercises:

Are you finding it difficult to get through meals? Be mindful and aware, both internally and externally. Check in with yourself; what's hindering you at meal times?

WHO'S TALKING—ED OR ME?

All through recovery I have been taught to go against ED. One way to do that is to make food choices based on what *I* want, not what ED wants. I noticed at times that my food choices leaned toward "healthier" choices rather than radical risky ones. In noticing this, I got scared for a minute. I began questioning myself. Was I ordering food based on caloric value again? Should I be worried? Am I doing something wrong?

At my next session with Thom, I posed the following questions to him regarding my thoughts. I asked, "Am I always supposed to pick the more radical food choice to prove that I am in recovery and going against ED? Should I be concerned about ordering a 'healthier' meal?"

Thom assured me that I do not have to always order a risky meal to prove anything. However, he also said I have to ask myself the question "who's talking?" In other words, when I am making a choice about what to have, I have to check in with myself to be sure it is Cheryl talking and not ED. I have to be true to myself and answer honestly.

After talking it out with Thom and recalling the many times I had to choose something, I realized that is was me talking and not ED. I was in control of what I was doing, not ED. I truly wanted what I was ordering and didn't base it on caloric value or a rule I used to live by.

As life happens and recovery becomes more mainstream in my life, I realize I am still learning to trust myself, my wants and desires, because I had done what ED wanted my entire life. I guess I just needed to be reassured that this brief fear I had is part of the recovery process—and it is.

<u>Recovery Tool:</u> Ask who's talking—ED or me?

<u>Recovery tools in chapter:</u> Talk therapy, honesty, trust

Reflections—Questions and Exercises:

Think about the last time you made a food choice. Who did you hear? Who was talking to you? Did you make the choice based on what you wanted or what ED wanted you to pick? Be true to yourself and recovery and answer honestly.

PUNCH A PILLOW

It was Saturday, and I woke up in a good mood. I had a cookout party to go to later in the day and was excited to see friends and meet new people. I decided to lie down and take a nap in the afternoon so I would be rested for the night ahead. (I knew I would be up much later than normal.) I awoke from my nap, made some coffee, and jumped in the shower. My mood seemed to be fine and nothing was off kilter or out of the ordinary—until I got dressed.

My bad body image took over and away it went. I put on an outfit and looked in the mirror, and I instantly tore myself apart. I started at my head and went all the way to my toes, picking apart everything in between. Off came that outfit and on went another and so too did the self-criticism. My insides were becoming knots while anger, frustration, and disgust filled my mind and spirit.

I realized what was happening and walked away from the mirror. I needed to get out some frustration and negative feelings, center myself and begin to think positively again, so I went to the bed and grabbed my pillow. I lifted it over my head and swung it down hard onto the bed a few times. Then I placed it on the bed and began to punch the center of it. Doing this released the frustration and negative feelings I was having about my body. It was a relief to get the feelings out. I then sat on the side of the bed and calmed myself down. I sang my body mantra and did some deep breathing. I held Moo Moo while I counted to fifty.

After ten minutes of using these various tools, I was able to calm myself down and tell myself, "I am not fat and these clothes fit me great. No matter what I put on, it will look great on me, and I'll be okay." I picked out an outfit and put it on. I did not look in the mirror when I was finished dressing. I knew that would only trigger me.

While in the car, I sang my body mantra, listened to music, did positive self-talk, and talked to Rachel to help me get out of the bad space I had just been in. I did not want the bad thoughts to have power over me. *I* wanted to be in control of my mood.

We got to the cookout and the night went off without a hitch. It was great to see my friends and hang out and laugh. People actually commented on what I was wearing and said how nice I looked. That was a true reality check.

Bad body image days still arise, but it is how I deal with them that is important. I realized what was happening to me, stepped aside, utilized some tools, and got through it. I did not let it affect my next meal or my night. I took the control back.

Recovery Tool: Punch a pillow

Recovery tools within the chapter: Body mantra, deep breathing, counting to fifty, tangible object, positive self-talk, talking with supports, music, friends

Reflections—Questions and Exercises:

What feelings come to the surface when you look in the mirror? Are they negative? If so, how do you release them? Let's get ahead of them. Write down three positive things you can say about yourself the next time you look in the mirror, like "I am beautiful, and I love and respect my new body." Write them down even if you don't believe them. The next time you face the mirror, say all of them. Do this each day, and soon you will see it's the truth.

TATTLE ON ED

Even though Thom and I have a great connection over the phone and work well together in that fashion, there is nothing like actually being in his presence and in his domain. There is something about seeing each other face-to-face that makes it feel so much more intense. I always want more because he makes me feel so strong, alive, and free. When I go to Nashville to work with Thom, I arrive on a Monday and have my sessions with him on Tuesday, Wednesday, and Thursday.

It was Tuesday morning, and I was getting ready for my day. I took out my clothes and started to get dressed. That's when ED decided to come out of his room, come downstairs, and stand right in front of me. As I pulled my pants up to my waist and fastened the button, ED began to tell me in a soft, soothing voice that my left leg was bigger than my right leg. He voice was so quiet and so serene, almost comforting. He proceeded to tell me my leg was bigger because I had eaten some food he did not approve of the day before and I had eaten a filling breakfast that morning.

He said to me, "Cheryl, what are you doing, have you forgotten everything I've been telling you your entire life? You need listen to me now, this is proof. Can you feel your leg? Look, your pants don't feel the same."

Immediately, I said (out loud), "Shut up ED, get out of here. I am trying to get dressed. Leave me alone!" He walked into another room and was mumbling the entire way there. I shook my head and said, "What a pest!"

Even though I am well into this process of recovery, ED never ceases to amaze me. I guess he figured since I was coming to see Thom, he would come along for the ride and rear his ugly head. I think ED wanted to show Thom that he was still lurking about and could strike at any time. ED wanted to prove a point, but could he? Not on my watch.

As I walked to Thom's office, ED came out of his room and talked in my ear. To stay strong, I talked back to him out loud walking along the roadway. My recovery voice was strong as I told ED, "ED, you are an annoying creature and I am not listening to you. I am going to see Thom and I don't want you around, so go to your room and get away from me." I forged ahead to my destination.

During my session with Thom, I brought up how ED was coming to me and what he was saying and how annoying he was being. Tattling on ED is a great recovery tool. Doing so depletes his power over you. You begin to take it back when you recognize what he may be trying to do. Acknowledging him to someone really ticks him off. He isn't a secret then; you expose him.

As Thom and I chatted, Thom clued me in on what ED was doing. He said, "ED is trying to hypnotize you into thinking your left leg is bigger than your right. He is telling you things over and over in a calming, soothing voice in the hope that your mind will think that way. Here, let me show you."

Thom instructed me to sit with my feet flat on the floor in a comfortable fashion. Then he told me to close my eyes, relax, and listen. So I sat there and listened to each word Thom said. I concentrated on his soothing, monotone voice as he told me to think about my left arm and how heavy it was. He proceeded to talk to me about my left arm, how it was heavier than my right, how it's like a weight against my leg. He was descriptive and soothing all at the same time.

He told me to open my eyes and said, "How do you feel?"

"Oh my gosh, my left arm feels so heavy," I said.

He asked me, "Do you really believe your left arm is now heavier than your right?"

"No," I said, "but it feels that way."

Then he said, "That is the power of hypnosis—and that is what ED is trying to do to you."

After I thought about it, I realized he was right. That was exactly the tactic ED was trying to use on me. He was trying to convince me of something that was untrue in a calming manner. I was ticked off that ED was trying to trick me. I thought, how dare he? Who does he think he's playing with? I'll show him! Thom told me to stay alert and keep going against ED. I was ready for him if he struck again. I'm in control, and I needed to remind ED of that fact.

As the day went on, ED tried again to hypnotize me. I told him, "ED, I know what you are trying to do and it won't work. As always, my power of intention is stronger than yours, so go away. Your tactic won't work. I figured it out and I'm stronger than you." After telling him this a few times, he understood I was not going to give in.

ED was aggravated and said with an attitude, "Fine, whatever! Have it your way!" and he walked away.

To help me keep him at bay, I went for a walk around Nashville and stopped by my favorite soda shop for lunch. I enjoyed my own company as I watched the locals go about their day. I had gotten through ED's sneak attack and had again let recovery take over. I was still winning, still feeling, and still living—all without ED.

Recovery Tool: Tattle on ED

Recovery tools within the chapter: Talking back to ED, distraction, going out to eat, talk therapy, following a meal plan

Reflections—Questions and Exercises:

Does ED sneak up on you when you least expect it? Is he trying to hypnotize or trick you? Describe how his voice sounds when sneaks. Where is he when he sneaks up on you? The next time you feel him trying to manipulate you, tell someone. How does it make you feel? List three things you can say or do to take your power back.

SECTION FOUR:
THE ESCAPE—
FINDING FREEDOM

BEING PRESENT

I had the afternoon to myself for a change—nothing to do, nowhere to go, no one to see. I had a book I could read, I could do some writing, go for a walk, or watch some TV. I decided to flip on the TV, and *Law and Order* was on (one of my favorite shows). I decided that just being present in the moment and chilling sounded great. So I tossed off my shoes and got cozy on the sofa.

As the TV show played and time went by, I realized something pretty amazing: I was actually able to just sit there and watch TV! Where was all the noise, where was the hell, where was the anxiety, where was the pain of just trying to relax? This was a wonderful, strange occurrence.

Not too long ago I could not "just sit" and watch TV without my mind racing and ED talking to me the entire time. I could never concentrate on a show and follow what was going on because ED was telling me I was a fat loser, that I was wasting my time, and that I needed to go do something that would benefit him, not me. ED used to blabber the whole time just to remind me that he was there. I could not get a moment's peace from him as thoughts of food, numbers, and rules occupied my head. I also had to be doing three things at once while trying to watch TV because my anxiety would not let me just sit.

That was my normal back when I was listening to ED. Now that I tell him to go to hell and go against what he says, I finally have some peace in my head. There is space and time to think. It's quiet and free. ED is just background noise; he is insignificant; he is a nobody, a nothing!

It is an amazing feeling to realize that I can just be and do without all the noise. Now that I have experienced it, I know how to find it again and can enjoy the moment and the freedom from ED's voice. I can enjoy my time. I can enjoy whatever I want to because I am free.

Recovery Tool: Being present

Recovery tools within the chapter: N/A

Reflections—Questions and Exercises:

Stop and listen. What do you hear? Sit in a quiet place and just be for five minutes. Close your eyes and focus on your breathing to calm your mind. Focus on the sounds and listen to what's around you. Take it all in, and then open your eyes. Write down what you heard. Did you find it soothing, relaxing, or anxiety provoking? Was it the hum of a light? Was it the voice of a friend? Was it the bark of a dog? Was it the chirp of a bird? What did you hear?

WEIGHT ACCEPTANCE

I was weighed at every appointment with Dr. G. My anxiety had significantly decreased about "the number," but I felt the need to do something more and bring this "weight thing" to another, healthier level. I didn't know how much I weighed (and still don't), but I was still anxious thinking about it and what it meant for me and my recovery. I wondered, is my weight too high, too low, or just right?

At my next appointment, I decided to ask Dr. G an important question. As I was getting dressed and she was typing my information into the computer, my heart started to beat a bit faster and my mouth started to go a little dry as I asked, "Dr. G, is my weight range the maximum I should ever weigh?" I stood on the other side of the curtain panicking, not knowing what she would say. I couldn't see her face, but I could hear it in her voice. Without hesitation she responded and said, "Um, no Cheryl. It's not."

With that response ED quickly tried to tell me that Dr. G was my enemy and she did not have my best interests in sight. ED told me Dr. G only wanted to get me fat, and I better not listen to anything she had to say. ED's been telling me that all along, so that was not anything new to my ears. I told him to be quiet and told him that Dr. G was a great doctor, that I trusted her and she knew what she was talking about. I told ED his advice on what to do was not wanted and told him to take a hike.

After ED's ramblings, I let recovery take charge to see where it would take me. Recovery told me Dr. G would never let me get fat and that Dr. G would always look out for me. It didn't matter if the number was higher than my weight range because Dr. G would keep an eye on me and keep me safe and healthy. Recovery told me to deepen the trust I had for my body and realize with absolute certainty it would not betray me. I did not have to be so cautious. With proper nourishment, I had to believe that my body would level out at a weight that was comfortable.

I sat with that for a while and came to a decision. With my decision came a shift in my thinking. I decided I would continue on the path of recovery and accept and fully trust the fact that my body will find its own true weight. I was going to be comfortable and let my body level out where it needs to in order to be healthy and happy. And it did.

I continued to avoid ED's advice and participated in healthy behaviors—and at my next appointment with Dr. G I didn't even ask if I was in range, out of range, or otherwise. It didn't matter. Not asking brings me one step closer to accepting my body and where it needs to be. If I get in trouble, I know Dr. G will let me know. Otherwise, I am going to love where I am and begin to get comfortable with my "true weight."

Recovery Tool: Acceptance

Recovery tools within the chapter: Talking back to ED, trust, listening for/to Recovery, keeping outpatient appointments

Reflections—Questions and Exercises:

It's hard to accept your true weight when you are going through it, but your body does end up where it should be when you are taking care of yourself and nourishing it. It naturally knows what to do. Write down three positive messages about you and your body (even if you don't believe them) and read them daily. You can write these on cards and carry them with you too. Example: I am strong, and my body is a vehicle I trust and love. Reading these messages to yourself helps with your acceptance and helps you fight back when ED tells you negative things.

EAT AND ENJOY A FEAR FOOD

It was a Tuesday morning and I was at work. I heard my cell phone beep to indicate I had received a text message. I looked down to see a message from my co-worker and friend, Sharon. The message read, "I got you a yummy treat." I knew instantly what she was bringing me—a Boston cream donut!

ED tried to worm his way in by telling me, "No way are you eating that thing." But Recovery chimed in right away and said, "You haven't had a donut recently so this will be a nice treat, and it's your favorite too." I continued with the positive self-talk and reframing until my morning snack arrived. My recovery voice dominated the conversation in my head, so ED was kept at bay. Under no circumstances was he to have the last word. *Never* let ED have the last word!

Sharon walked in with the bag in her hand and—lo and behold—she had a Boston cream donut, all for me. We sat together at our desks and had our morning snack. We talked and laughed as we drank our coffee and ate our donuts, just like regular folks. I enjoyed every minute and savored every bite of it.

Not too long ago ED would have taken over, and I would not have eaten that donut. I would have gone into full-fledged panic mode, gotten ticked off, and would have thought of any excuse not to eat it. ED would have won that battle. But those days are over. Today I am in charge! Today I can allow myself to have any treat and can recognize that a treat is something delicious and decadent, something I add to life, not a deprivation.

I've come a long way. Not only did I eat the donut and enjoy it, my friend felt comfortable enough to get one for me. Sharon and I have been friends for seventeen years, so she knows all too well the craziness that comes along with ED. In the past, she would not have bought me a donut for fear I would yell at her and have an attitude the rest of the day—all because of ED. Today, Sharon can see how far I have come and is confident of getting a good (and normal) response to her nice gestures.

<u>Recovery Tool:</u> Eat a fear food

<u>Recovery tools within the chapter:</u> Listen for/to Recovery, positive self-talk, talking with supports, laughter, eating with a support

Reflections—Questions and Exercises:

When was the last time you enjoyed a yummy treat with a friend? Write down five yummy treats that you want to share with a friend. Perhaps it's a favorite of yours or perhaps it's something from childhood. Show ED who's boss: Call up a friend and plan a time to get together to enjoy a yummy treat. Remember, there is no such thing as bad food—all food is okay! You deserve it. You are worth it.

POSITIVE MANTRA

I made plans with a friend I had not seen for many months. I have known this person for years, and she is well aware of my struggles with anorexia. After I set up a time to get together, I started to prepare myself because this friend has a remarkable knack for saying "interesting statements." She means no harm, and I love her, but in the past her statements had been well received by ED. He took them and ran with them. For example, one time she told me that a dress I was wearing made me look heavy. ED took that comment and told me I was fat and ugly and that I needed to restrict and exercise so people would be able to look at me without disgust. Back then, I listened to him and did what he said; but not now.

The day came and I felt strong and was prepared for whatever might come out of her mouth. I waited with anticipation. Well, there we were enjoying each other's company, and BAM— out it came: She said, "Compared to what you looked liked before, you look overweight!"

As I leaned back into the booth, my eyes were wide as her words hit the air and then rolled around in my head. Within the next second, ED and Recovery were screaming at the same time, trying to see who could get to me first. They were in a fight to see who could grab my attention. I heard them both.

ED was saying, "See, she is right, your friend wouldn't lie to you, you are fat. You looked so much better before. You need to lose some weight, and I can help you do it."

Recovery was saying, "She's right, before you were sick and unhealthy and now you are healthy and alive. You look great, and she is a good friend for noticing how your hard work is paying off."

I had a decision to make right then and there. Who was I going to listen to? That decision would affect the rest of my day and/or days. Would I let the simple words of a friend have a negative effect of me? Would I give ED the power or would I give Recovery the power? Before, ED would have won the fight for my attention, and I would have run to unhealthy behaviors. I would have done what he said, how he said it, and it would have put me deeper into the black hole of death and despair. Not now.

I chose to listen to Recovery. I had worked too hard at keeping ED away from me, and I was not going to let anything get in the way. I decided to chuckle at the statement my friend made and view it as a recovery statement. I tossed any potential negativity of it aside. I continued to say positive statements about myself and my progress, so ED would not have the chance to sneak in and take me away. I said to myself, "I am not overweight, I am healthy and happy" over and over.

People say silly things, and it is our reaction to them that decides where we will go from there. We have a choice in how we react. I choose to react with recovery in mind.

Recovery Tool: Positive mantra

Recovery tools within the chapter: Listen for/to Recovery, following a meal plan, socializing, eating with supports

Reflections—Questions and Exercises:

If a friend that you love and trust said the same statement to you, what would Recovery say? Write down three statements that Recovery would say to be sure you would follow its lead. Then write down a mantra that you could say over and over to yourself for positive reinforcement.

REJOIN SOCIETY

When I was in the depths of my eating disorder, my strength and drive to do anything was nonexistent. I only wanted to be alone with ED and wanted to be away from everything and everyone. ED had convinced me that I only needed him and him alone, and ED was the one I chose to go to.

As my recovery began, I slowly came of out isolation and rejoined the world around me. Being out in the world again felt like I was exposing myself. The security blanket around me was slowly coming off, and people were looking. I could see them and they could see me. I didn't have ED to hide behind. I wondered, will people like me? Will I be fun to go out with? Can I really do this? Who am I? Am I a good friend? I was uncomfortable but knew deep inside I must do this to move forward and get back an important part of my life.

Now I find myself doing things I never did before. Whether it's running around doing errands, going out to dinner with friends (a feat in itself), or being spontaneous (which was never the case before recovery), I have the physical strength, emotional strength, and drive to do things and be with people. Recovery has given that to me.

I never realized how much of my time was focused on ED until ED began to slowly disappear and I filled it with other, healthy things. My calendar is always full, whether it be fun or relaxation, and I am enjoying living each day. More important, *I* am in control of my life's calendar, not ED. I showed him who's boss—ME!

<u>Recovery Tool:</u> Rejoin society

<u>Recovery tools within the chapter:</u> Eating with supports, socializing, going out to eat, following a meal plan

Reflections—Questions and Exercises:

Living life without ED is amazing and free and possible for everyone. When you plan your day, who is in control of your calendar? Write down what an ED-free day would look like for you. Where would you go, what would you do, and what would you nourish yourself with? After you write it, read it and know that you can achieve that day. It's within your reach.

ME TIME

At the end of a session with Bob, there I was, sitting on the recliner right across from him. As I looked up, I saw he had a small smirk on his face. His face made me feel like he was going to say something important. The words he spoke took me by surprise. He said, "You've earned it. I'll see you in two weeks." It took me a minute to actually realize what he was saying. For many years, I had gone to individual therapy every week and sometimes more frequently. Now I was being told I could take a break—a week off. I heard what he had said, but it took me a minute to react.

I smiled at him and said, "What? I don't have to come back here for two weeks?"

He smiled and said, "Yes."

I was floored and amazed. The concept was new to me. Honestly, fear overcame me for a moment because I had never been without therapy. I asked myself, will I be able to go that long without therapy? Will I be okay? I wanted to snap right back to Bob and say, "NO, I'm not ready to take a break." But I realized that he was giving me something I had earned and something I needed.

Bob said that I had done such hard work and made great progress, so I deserved some extra "Cheryl time"—time to do new things, fun things, anything I wanted—time to live! He also reminded me that my "Cheryl time" had already increased greatly because I wasn't spending my time with ED. I wasn't obsessing about rules or participating in eating disorder behaviors. I was learning to live free. I had reclaimed my time from ED. I had taken it back.

So on my regularly scheduled therapy night, there I was, sitting in a restaurant and having dinner with friends (I thought ED would love to see that!). We were chatting up a storm, laughing so hard our bellies hurt and having a great time. I was thrilled to have the extra time to myself. It felt weird, but Thom has always told me that "feeling weird equals doing good." So I went with it.

A few months passed, and I was getting use to having the extra "Cheryl time." Well, who would have guessed that I would get more time handed to me on a silver tray? Soon enough Bob said, "I'll see you in three weeks."

I smiled right back at him and without hesitation I said, "Three, great, I'll see you in three!"

As I got further along in recovery and the work I was doing showed, it was no longer necessary for me to have a weekly appointment. As I healed, I earned more time for myself to live the life I had once lost to ED. Life itself is therapy, and you learn lessons from living it.

I love my newfound free time. I do what I want and enjoy every minute of it. Sometimes I choose to go out with friends or family and other times I just sit home and vegetate. No matter what I choose to fill the time, I realize I deserve it and have earned it. The most important thing is it's "Cheryl time," *not* ED's!

Recovery Tool: Me time

Recovery tools within the chapter: Talk therapy, going out to eat, socializing, eating with supports, following a meal plan, laughter

Reflections—Questions and Exercises:

As you get stronger and stronger and move forward in recovery and further away from ED, you too will earn free time. What activities will you do to fill your "me time"? Will you go to dinner with friends, go to the movies, go shopping? List five things you would like to do (without ED) when you have your "me time." When "your time" happens, pull out your list and begin to cross them off one by one!

SELF-ACCEPTANCE

My birthday was coming up and I wanted to celebrate my newfound life. I wanted to do something that would show off the new me. I wanted people to see on the outside what I was finally feeling on the inside. I came up with the perfect day: a makeover in New York City. I had always wanted to get my hair done in a famous salon, and my birthday would be the perfect time. So I found a salon, made an appointment, and waited for the day to arrive.

I was so excited. I could not wait for the day to get here. I decided to give the salon free reign with my hair. I wanted a haircut and color that matched my face and body and my personality. I thought, I wonder what I will look like?

The day finally came and I could not contain my excitement. There I was in the Big Apple, ready for the new me. I opened the door to the salon and was amazed. It was beautiful. It had multiple levels, and stylists, colorists, and manicurists were all around. The salon was done in silver and blue. A circular sofa was in the front for the clients to relax and wait. Cappuccinos were being sipped all around, and attendants were waiting on the clients' every need. It was amazing. I had never seen so many people working at a salon before. They were all dressed in black pants and white shirts. Every chair in the salon was full.

My colorist, Clark, came to get me. He was tall, bald, and muscular. He brought me to the second floor and showed me to a chair. He ran his fingers through my hair to check out what he was dealing with. "Nice color," he said. He looked at my skin tone and the color I already had and determined he would keep the brown. He said he would do a gloss and give me a few highlights to break up the brown. I was a bit disappointed because I was going to get the same color but told myself he was the expert.

Then Robert, my hairstylist, came over. He was tall with dark hair and brown eyes. He asked me a couple of questions about my current style, my routine, and my desires. I told him he could do what he wanted and that I was open to change and new things. He played with my hair and told me he would like to cut a bit off the back and cut the sides to give it some style.

I said, "Great, let's get started."

And so it began. Clark applied color to my hair, then gloss was added, then the highlights. I couldn't tell what the color looked like because it was wet, but I was excited nonetheless. The first step was completed.

Next I moved on to Robert. As I sat in his chair, my heart skipped a beat and I was filled with excitement. I couldn't wait to see what he would do and how I would look. I was ready. He combed out my hair and began cutting a little bit here and there. I was excited to see what would transpire. After a few cuts, he said, "I've changed my mind. I'm going to texture your hair and leave the bulk of it the way it is." Inside I was very disappointed but out loud I said, "Okay, you're the expert."

After the cut was finished he took the blow-dryer and brush to my hair. He was drying it in a way that I would never be able to do at home. He was doing it the "salon way." He informed me that all I had to do to "do" my hair on a daily basis was to push it around with my fingers while blow-drying it, and I would be all set. My hair would fall into place and look beautiful. I wasn't so convinced.

After he was done, I was excited to see the final outcome. My belly was doing flips as he turned the chair around to the mirror. I looked up, and to my surprise, I looked exactly the same. I said an appropriate "thank you" but was very disappointed. I thought, I came all this way for *this*? My friend that was with me raved about how nice my hair looked and how different it was, but I knew she was just being nice. I knew it didn't look that much different. I was looking for the wow factor and didn't get it.

The day after I returned home, I had a session with Thom. I was telling him all about my birthday and what I did and how disappointed I was. I told him about how I wanted this big change and I didn't get it.

After listening to my story, Thom said something that made me think and took me for a loop. He said, "Cheryl, you already had what you were seeking. Nothing needs to change. You already look like you need to look."

It took a minute to wrap my brain around what he was saying, but I understood it. I just had a hard time believing it. Sometimes my self-esteem doesn't match the truth.

Coming to the realization that I am perfectly fine the way I am was the perfect birthday present. I was searching for something that I had all along. I just had to remind myself of that fact and actually look at and within myself.

I went into work that Monday and everyone said, "You don't look any different. What happened to the makeover?"

My reply was, "Apparently, I'm fine just the way I am."

Their response to that was, "We could have told you that!"

My gift to myself was more than I imagined getting. It was the best present I received, and I will have it forever!

<u>Recovery Tool:</u> Self-acceptance

<u>Recovery tools within the chapter:</u> Friends, self-care, talk therapy

Reflections—Questions and Exercises:

We tend to go through life only looking at ourselves from the outside. Sit in a quiet place and look at yourself from the inside out. What do you see? What do you feel? What present can you give yourself? Look inside. Write down five positive words about yourself and read them out loud. Are you loyal, honest, friendly, pretty? In the end, *you* are the best gift you can give yourself.

LIVE BY A HEALTHY RULE

As I mentioned in a previous chapter ("Transforming ED's Rules"), one of ED's rules for me was that I was not allowed to weigh enough to give blood. He told me that if I weighed enough to give blood, then I was a fat failure and a disappointment to him. Through recovery I have learned how to transform those rules and live by my new ones. I make those new recovery rules/statements a part of who I am and what I do.

One day I was driving home from work and saw a sign for a blood drive. When I read that sign I remembered the rule ED once told me. As I drove down the street, I knew what I had to do and why. I decided to stick another nail in ED's coffin and live by my rule, not his. I knew I was healthy enough to do it and nothing could stop me. I can decide, and I have the power. I decided I would do it; I would donate blood.

The day came, and I felt proud of the decision I had made. In taking care of myself and going against ED, I now had the ability to help others in their fight for life. My action of donating would help others to live.

I parked my car, walked inside, and checked in at the table. ED tried to sneak in front of me and whispered, "Cheryl, if they accept your blood, it means you are fat."

I rolled my eyes, shook my head in disgust at ED and said, "whatever" and continued on. I knew he was lying. Everything ED says is a lie.

I filled out the paperwork, answered the questions, had the necessary tests, and was on my way to donating. My chest was full of pride as I walked to the table because I knew where I had come from and where I was now. As I lay down on the table and the nurse stuck me with the needle, I envisioned the needle sticking ED and said to myself, hey ED, how does that feel? It made me smile to know I was causing him pain.

As I lay there with the blood bag attached to my arm, feelings of pride, strength, and courage ran through my body. At one time I had needed to be saved, and by leaving ED and following recovery, I was now healthy and strong enough to save my life as well as other lives. No one else in that room realized the pain and struggle I had to go through to get to where I was that day, but I knew!

That blood drive was my first, and it will not be my last. It was one of many firsts because I choose to live my life free from ED.

Recovery Tool: Live by a healthy rule

Recovery tools within the chapter: Talking back to ED

Reflections—Questions and Exercises:

It's empowering to do things that ED once told you that you couldn't do. It shows ED who is boss and who is in control—YOU. What will one of your firsts be? List five things that you will do that ED once told you can't. Show him you mean business and do them. Feel the power behind your actions.

ACCEPTING COMPLIMENTS

It was a Thursday afternoon and the sun was shining. I was well rested and in a jovial mood. The week was coming to an end, and the talk around the office was about everybody's weekend plans. I sat at my desk, engrossed in what I was doing. I could hear someone bustling around me, but I wasn't paying attention to who it was.

A few minutes passed and I looked up to see Lou, our plant man. Lou has been taking care of our office plants for many years and comes to see us on a weekly basis. As usual, he stopped at my desk and we chatted about our weekend plans and the goings-on of the current week. As he was talking to me, his head tilted sideways, his eyebrows went up, and a smirk came over his face.

"What is it, Lou? Is everything okay?" I asked.

"I am just noticing something," he replied.

"What is it?" I said.

"I have to say, Cheryl—you just look so healthy and vibrant," he replied.

His words came at me from out of the blue. I replied with a simple "Thanks, Lou."

Lou has no idea about ED and the struggles I have gone through. He is simply a person who has seen me on a weekly basis for years. His words were genuine and meant a lot to me. In the past, Lou's words would have been like a stab in the heart. ED would have told me that I let myself go and that I am fat. He would have given me specific instructions on how to "fix myself." ED always told me that healthy equals fat, which I now know is a lie.

I now have the tools to keep ED quiet. I speak before he can. I control my words and actions. Today, I can listen to Lou's words and take them as the compliment he intended.

Lou's words (and his noticing) are the icing on the cake. I work hard in recovery, and it is nice to know my hard work is paying off. It is showing from the inside out. I truly am healthy and vibrant.

<u>Recovery Tool:</u> Hear and accept compliments

<u>Recovery tools within the chapter:</u> Socializing

Reflections—Questions and Exercises:

Hearing and accepting the kind words people tell you helps you realize who you are and how hard you have worked at recovery. Ask a trusted support to sit with you and give you compliments—to tell you all the things they love about you—while you hear each one, accept it, and then say thank you. Afterward, write down what your support told you and keep it close to you for a reality reminder.

RECOVERY REFLECTIONS

One night I babysat for my friends Shelia and Mike. Their daughter Gabriella was three months old. I do not have any children, so I was excited to see her and play with her, to hold her and care for her. I love kids.

Gabriella and I watched a baby video, did some baby exercises, and played with toys. After all of the activity, it was dinner time. She was getting fussy and was definitely telling me it was time to eat. I prepared her bottle and sat down to feed her. As I held her, she was lying there with her arms and legs totally relaxed and spread out, and her belly was extended and relaxed. She was enjoying her dinner and was very content.

As she lay there, I thought about how lucky I am that I am healthy enough to be trusted to watch this beautiful being. There was a time when ED had such control over me that I was out of control and had lost my ability to truly function in life. People were afraid of my fragility and my lack of concentration and so on. Now I have the strength, attentiveness, and willingness to be responsible for another life. The thought of trying to babysit when I was so sick gives me chills down my spine because something bad could have happened in a split second. I am so happy with all that recovery has given me.

I was also thinking about how Gabriella was so comfortable in the skin she was in. She was lying there with her extended baby belly hanging out for the world to see. She did not have a care in the world and was without self-judgment. I thought about my life and when I began judging myself. I was so young. And today I work so hard at trying not to judge myself. Seeing Gabriella just being in the moment without judgment was comforting and brought more hope into my soul. I asked myself, why can't I be like that and adopt that thinking all the time? What is stopping me? I realized the answer was "nothing."

I also thought about how Gabriella put her trust in me to get what she needs. I thought about how I had to learn to trust my treatment team and myself to get what I needed—to trust them to tell me what was best for me and trust myself to believe it.

Being with Gabriella was refreshing; she was so innocent and alive. It reminded me that life is out there for the taking and anything is possible. Being healthy in mind and spirit is a true gift. I am grateful for the gift of recovery. Recovery has given me the ability and power to view the world as Gabriella does.

Recovery Tool: Reflection

Recovery tools within the chapter: N/A

Reflections—Questions and Exercises:

Look back through your recovery process. What vision has recovery given you? What have you noticed is different now than it was before? Make a list of things that recovery has given you. You'll be surprised by how many things you will come up with.

GIVE BACK

When I was listening to ED, I had limited ability to be there for anyone if they needed me. I could barely help myself or get out of my own way, let alone help anyone else. I stuck with ED, thinking he would help me live a better life and allow me to be who I wanted to be. Boy, was I wrong. He did nothing of the sort. He only provided me with torture, misery, and despair. Fortunately, I found the hope and strength to move away from ED and have realized who I am and what I can become. Thanks to recovery, I have found a better life. Today I share my triumphant story of hope through this book and speaking engagements, yet I recently discovered that I had a longing to do even more.

To help me with that, I looked to my friend Shannon Cutts. Shannon is the author of *Beating Ana: How to Outsmart Your Eating Disorder and Take Your Life Back* and is the founder of Key to Life and Mentor Connect (www.key-to-life.com). Mentor Connect is a program that connects people who need eating disorder recovery support ("mentees") with those who have received help themselves and now want to offer it to others ("mentors"). I spoke with Shannon about becoming involved in Mentor Connect and immediately signed up to become a volunteer mentor. My heart was ready to help guide a sufferer to freedom.

I took on two mentees and talk to them daily. We brainstorm for ways to help keep them in the recovery mindset. They look to me for guidance and suggestions as they fight ED. We talk about daily struggles, fears, recovery tools, and visions for the future. I am their confidante and friend, and they are not alone. They have a connection to someone who understands their pain and struggles and who has made it through to the other side to achieve lasting recovery.

Having these relationships also helps me along my continued path of recovery. Helping them reminds me of where I came from and all the pain I left behind. It reminds me why I want recovery and continues to give me the strength to move forward. It saddens me to hear their struggles and despair because I want to take all their pain away, but I know that I can't. Recovery is a process—one that must be gone through step by step if it is to last. I remind them that in the end, it's all worth it.

My entire being is healthy and alive thanks to recovery and because of it I can help bring recovery into the lives of others who are struggling.

Helping someone who is where I was and who wants to be where I am makes me happy and gives me a sense of purpose. When I was with ED, I had no purpose and I never found the happiness I was looking for. Now that I have found recovery, happiness follows me everywhere, and I have the strength and ability to give back.

__Recovery Tool:__ Share recovery knowledge (give back)

__Recovery tools within the chapter:__ Support

Reflections—Questions and Exercises:

Recovery gives you strength and knowledge. Are you ready, strong enough, and willing to offer your support to others? List three ways that you might give others support and how it would help you in your recovery.

CREATE/REDISCOVER
FOOD TRADITIONS

I am a Boston Red Sox fan and have had the pleasure of attending many games over the years. Fenway Park is a great place to bring the family to see a game. Recently I've been fortunate enough to enjoy a few games at the park with my niece Stephanie, who's twelve, and my nephew Stephen, who's eleven.

One day at the park my niece and I were walking around checking out the sights and watching batting practice. As we maneuvered around the other spectators, we passed a stand for fried dough.

I impulsively said, "Oh my gosh, I love fried dough."

"I love fried dough too!" my niece replied.

I promised her that we would get some during the game. Back in our seats, we watched the game until our craving got the better of us. At the fifth inning, we looked at each other and said, "Fried dough!" We walked down to the stand and ordered. We put our toppings on it and took a bite before heading back our seats. It was so good.

A few weeks later, we were on the way to another game together, reminiscing about the previous game, the fried dough, and the fun we had. So, in the fifth inning we looked at each other and said, "Fried dough!" We marched down to the stand, placed our order, and took a bite—just like before and just as yummy.

A few weeks later at yet another game, we looked at each other during the fifth inning and said, you guessed it—fried dough! On our way to the stand, my niece said, "Auntie, this is becoming our new tradition."

"Stephanie, you are exactly right," I laughed. "Let's call it Fried Dough at Fenway!" And thereby a tradition was born—and a delicious one at that!

Before recovery, ED would have never even let me think about fried dough, let alone say out loud that I loved it, let alone eat it! He would have stopped those thoughts immediately. He would have berated me and told me I was too fat and that fried dough would make me fatter. He would have also told me I was weak if I ate it.

Today, recovery takes over and squashes ED's voice before he can get a word out. I stay in the moment and enjoy this new tradition with my niece—no guilt allowed. I know that we are making memories together. ED cannot and will not ever take that away from me again. I won't let him.

Forming traditions around food is a normal part of human culture. Our traditions are usually based around family and food and making memories from them. ED's presence takes away that ability. Recovery gives it all back to you and then some. Because of recovery, I can welcome new food traditions or reconnect with old ones and realize it's all a normal part of healthy living.

<u>Recovery Tool:</u> Create/rediscover food traditions

<u>Recovery tools within the chapter:</u> Family, fun activities, laughter, eating with supports

Reflections—Questions and Exercises:

What are some traditions that you once enjoyed? How does ED stand in your way of participating in those or forming new ones? Write down three ways that you can push ED aside and get back to those traditions that you love—and also make new ones.

ATTEND RECOVERY EVENTS

My local eating disorder association, MEDA (www.medainc.org), holds a yearly fundraiser; one year they honored my doctor, Dr. Suzanne Gleysteen. Without hesitation, I knew I wanted to go and honor this person whom I love and respect, who has helped save my life and continues to do so.

I was nervously excited because I knew that many of the healthcare providers I had met through treatment and beyond would be there. Seeing them in a social setting would be interesting. I wondered if any of them would remember me. On the day of the gala my hair was done, my makeup was on, and my gown looked great on me (thanks, Recovery!). I was ready to go.

Rachel and I arrived at the gala and walked into a room filled with over 200 people mingling. Right as we walked in, we were met with a familiar face. After catching up, we walked around the room to get a feel for who was there and the auction items available.

I saw Dr. G right away and gave her my congratulations. She looked so beautiful and so happy. She thanked us for being there. Next I saw Bob, and we exchanged hellos as well. While walking around, I saw the faces of the many people who had helped me in my recovery. To my surprise, a few of them remembered me. I was honored. It was great to catch up with them, thank them, and give them an update on what was going on with me.

During dinner, speeches given by the MEDA staff and invited guests echoed throughout the room. The passion in their voices was evident. It was a very nurturing atmosphere. I sat there as a proud recipient of the support the staff at MEDA and the other professionals in attendance give sufferers.

After dinner, a representative of MEDA introduced Dr. G with a grand introduction, one she deserves. Everyone stood up and cheered before she even spoke a word. The overwhelming support and gratitude in the room was exhilarating. It was electric. As Dr. G spoke, my heart was filled with honor and appreciation for this woman who helped saved my life. The work she does to help people with eating disorders is extraordinary.

As I listened, a sense of overwhelming pride came over me. There I was—a survivor. I was in a room filled with people who care and, specifically, with individuals who helped me survive. I have never felt such a feeling of accomplishment and pride before. It was new to me. I could feel it deep down. All my hard work had paid off. I did it—I am doing it—I am living my life free from ED. Thank you everyone. I have arrived!

<u>Recovery Tool:</u> Attend recovery events

<u>Recovery tools within the chapter:</u> Socializing, following a meal plan, laughter, eating with supports

Reflections—Questions and Exercises:

What fills you with a sense of pride? Is it attending a recovery event, eating a fear food, being able to communicate, or seeking treatment? Think about yourself and your recovery, and list three things that fill you with pride.

GIVE THANKS

I woke up this past Thanksgiving Day with excitement running through my veins. I was going to see my family and spend the day with them. After breakfast, I showered and got ready for my day. I was looking forward to seeing my niece and nephew. With Tupperware in hand for any leftovers, we arrived at my parents' house just after noon.

My family and I were all gathered in a warm home with love filling the air. The aroma of turkey and Mom's stuffing filled the house. We chatted about daily life and the upcoming Christmas season as we waited for the dinner bell to ring.

We sat down to a hot meal with family gathered all around the table. Laughter filled the room as we took bite after bite. We caught up on all the family gossip and reminisced about the old days. We finished dinner, cleaned up, and moved to the living room to relax.

My nephew asked me, "Auntie Cheryl, will you play checkers with me?"

"Of course I will," I replied.

We sat at the table for half an hour, played checkers, and belly laughed. It was great to see him sitting across from me smiling, laughing, and enjoying himself. He legitimately beat me a few times too. This time with him was special to me because I was spending quality time with family and making memories. I wasn't beating myself up over what I ate or using a negative behavior to get through a feeling. I was enjoying the moment, relaxing and being in the now. This is what Thanksgiving is all about—family and memories, not food.

There was a time when Thanksgiving Day brought me nothing but anxiety, panic, stress, and fear. I feared seeing the food, feared eating it, and dreaded having to see everyone. From Thanksgiving to New Year's I was one big anxiety-filled ball, and I could not break free from it. I obsessed about everything—calories, food, parties, people, and presents. You name it, I obsessed about it. My brain did not get a moment's peace. It was constantly on the go.

The holidays have such a different meaning for me now that I am in recovery. Now I can enjoy the holidays and let food take the back seat. The company I keep and the memories I make during the holidays is what is important to me and what I see first—and ED is not invited. The food is literally just filler.

On Thanksgiving Day and every day I give thanks for my recovery and am grateful I am alive to enjoy each moment and experience new things. I know I am safe because I disobey ED, surround myself with supports, and nourish myself. Now the holidays bring me joy, not pain.

<u>Recovery Tool:</u> Give thanks

<u>Recovery tools within the chapter:</u> Following a meal plan, playing games, laughter, family, eating with supports

Reflections—Questions and Exercises:

At Thanksgiving, we reflect on things that we are thankful for, like family, friends, good health, or a good job. Being in recovery allows you to see and appreciate things you never could before because ED was in the way. Push ED aside right now and list five things that you are thankful for in your life. To keep the positive recovery momentum going, keep a gratitude journal and list five things each night that you are thankful for.

SOCIALIZING

I sat in front of my computer and double-clicked to open an email: it was a date, Friday would be girls' night out. I was excited. When I was with ED, girls' night out didn't happen. Isolation was more like it. ED used to tell me that I only needed him, and I believed him. Now I go against ED, listen to Recovery, and go hang out with friends.

We were going to meet at the restaurant at 7 PM. This would be new for me because I had never been to this particular restaurant before. I was excited for it. When I was with ED, I hardly ever ventured out to a restaurant, and if I did, I never went to a new restaurant. I only went to places where I knew the menu and knew what to order. With recovery, I can go where I want.

After work on Friday I went home, took care of the dogs, and freshened up a bit before leaving. I put on my new black jeans, a red shirt, and black boots. I felt good about myself and looked in the mirror before I left.

"Damn, I look good!" I said.

That was a statement that ED never let me say. He used to pick me apart piece by piece until I ended up crying and feeling horrible about myself. Not now. Now I can look at myself and see that I do look good—and what's more important, I feel good.

I pulled into the parking lot, found a space, and parked the car. It was cold outside and the wind was blowing, so I hurried across the lot and made my way to the door. I was so excited to see everyone. I walked into the lobby and saw everyone sitting there.

"Hey, girls," I said.

Everyone got up and we all exchanged hugs and hellos. We told the hostess we were ready to be seated. She brought us to a round table in the corner of the room, a perfect place to chat and catch up. The waitress handed us menus and told us the specials. I was interested to see what this place had to offer. I grabbed my menu and opened it up. We were all talking and joking as we each looked at our menus to decide what we wanted to eat. Recovery has given me the ability to look at a menu and engage in conversations with friends at the same time. Before recovery, I would have been engrossed in the menu as I obsessed about the food, the calories, the portion size, wondering what others would be getting, and so on. Now, I am able to look and talk at the same time without anxiety. I was impressed with the menu. The choices were plenty and new dishes caught my eye. I couldn't wait to try something new. I always make it a point to try new dishes to expand my food horizons. Food variety is important because I don't want to fall into the trap of safety foods. It's fun and enjoyable to try new foods and dishes I've never had before. Variety is the spice of life! Today, I am able to walk into any restaurant (or friend's home) and order off the menu without panic, fear, rules, or judgment. After a few minutes, the waitress came and took our order. I couldn't wait to dig in.

Our girls' night out continued with laugh after laugh. At times we were so loud that the other patrons stared at us—but we didn't care! It was great to see each other and be together. Being with friends, loving and accepting myself, having fun and trying new things are some of the experiences that recovery has shown me. I can appreciate it and welcome it. I don't fear it any longer.

<u>Recovery Tool:</u> Socializing

<u>Recovery tools within the chapter:</u> Positive self-talk, going out to eat, following a meal plan, laughter, eating new foods, friends, eating with supports

Reflections—Questions and Exercises:

Going out with friends is a normal activity in daily life that is fun and enjoyable. What have been your experiences during a girls' night out? Is there anything you didn't get a chance to do that you would like because ED stood in your way? What steps could you take to push ED aside? What would you do differently next time?

SUPPORT

I went to Club Med in Mexico on vacation and discovered they have a circus there. Part of this circus was a trapeze. I have always wanted to do that but never had the chance. There I sat on the bleachers in ninety-degree heat with the sun blazing down on me and watched people climb up, climb over to the platform, jump off, and go. I'm deathly afraid of heights, so I wasn't sure if I would have the guts to go through with it. I made a snap decision and decided to go for it.

I got up from the bleachers and got my instructions from the trainer. My stomach was doing nervous flips as I listened to her tell me the dos and don'ts of the trapeze. I wasn't sure if the beads of sweat on my brow were from the sun or from my nerves as I walked over to the ladder.

I said my good-byes to the folks on the ground and began climbing up the wobbly, two-feet wide, four-story ladder. As I climbed, I looked straight ahead so I could see the ocean. I figured it would help me be less afraid if I could see something so beautiful. Well, it didn't work so well. Fear overcame me as I stopped on my way up and said out loud, "I can't do this. I'm scared." Friends down below and the other people there cheered me on and sent positive thoughts my way. "You can do it, Cheryl," they shouted. "Just put one foot in front of the other and climb."

I was paralyzed with fear as I stood on the ladder. I wondered, should I continue to climb up or should I get down? As I stood there and pondered that question, Recovery actually stepped in and said, "Cheryl, you found the strength inside of you to fight off ED and be in recovery, so climbing this ladder will be a piece of cake. You can do it."

I said to myself, "I can totally do this. I am in recovery, and in recovery I can do anything." And so I did. One step at a time, I reached the top. I got my footing, grabbed that trapeze, and flew through the air. It was so much fun.

Like recovery, I had the support there to help me keep going and reach my goal. Having support around you to help you beat your eating disorder is vital. It gives you the courage, guidance, and strength to keep going. Without the support of my friends, family, and treatment team, I would not be here today. Support is an important part of helping us reach our goals. Seek out the support around you that will help you climb to the top. You can do it. Just put one foot in front of the other.

<u>Recovery Tool:</u> Support

<u>Recovery tools within the chapter:</u> Positive self-talk, listen for/to Recovery, friends, taking risks

Reflections—Questions and Exercises:

Overcoming fears makes us stronger in life and in our recovery. It gives us the ability to see how far we have come, what we have accomplished, and how hard we have worked. Make a list of fears that have you overcome in your recovery. Are there more you want to overcome? List those as well and then list the steps you can take to overcome them. You can do it....one step at a time!

AFTERWORD

Life goes on and so does the growth and strength of my recovery. Recovery for me is a journey, not a destination—and I honor, celebrate, and respect every minute of it. Recovery gives me the ability to live freely and be who I am all without ED. I learn more about myself each day and welcome with open arms every feeling and every emotion that goes along with it. I can now say that *I* am in control of my life, every aspect of it. There are no rules, no guilt, no despair or shame, just freedom, honesty, joy, and beauty. I am finally free; ED has been silenced.

Sure, I have my days of stress, anger, lack of sleep, and anxiety. That's normal; that's life. It's how I chose to deal with it all that matters. I follow the path of recovery. I don't go to ED to make me feel better because he can't do any such thing. *I* am in control of my reactions, my world, and my destiny.

Recovery can be yours. You have the power of will and the choice to break free from the behaviors, obsessive thoughts, struggle, pain, depression, and feelings of despair. With recovery, it all gets better. You begin to heal from the inside out and truly see who you are without ED. "You" are in there and "you" deserve to come out and live in freedom.

Remember this: ED takes and Recovery gives!

My hope for you is that you will find the light and strength that is inside of you and use it to guide your way to freedom. Take what you like from the pages you've read and weave it into your own recovery process and see what grows. Show ED that *you* are the boss—and tell him you don't need him any more. Tell ED NO! You CAN do this. You have the strength. If I can do it, you can too.

Recovery is there for the taking. Reach out and take it by the hand and see where it leads you. You will be amazed at all the places you will go. Freedom awaits!

Breinigsville, PA USA
18 March 2010
234399BV00002B/2/P